BOOMING BRANDS

Harsh Pamnani is a renowned business storyteller and brand expert. He partners with businesses to develop powerful story banks—curated collections of compelling stories that leaders can use in both internal and external communications to grow their mindshare and market share. He has authored several best-selling books and articles on brand building, which have appeared in top-tier publications like *CNBC*, *Forbes*, *The Economic Times* and *The Financial Express*.

Harsh has worked with a range of organisations, from unicorn startups like FirstCry and Icertis, to think tanks like the World Bank and TiE, to corporates like Deloitte, Cognizant and HSBC.

Harsh has shared his expertise and experience through speaking engagements at prestigious institutions like TEDx (six times), Josh Talks, IIT Bombay and IIM Ahmedabad. He teaches startup branding at MICA Ahmedabad.

Harsh is an alumnus of XLRI, Jamshedpur and IET-DAVV, Indore. For more information about Harsh and his work, please visit www.harshpamnani.com. You can get in touch with him via email at harshpamnani@hotmail.com or connect with him on LinkedIn at https://www.linkedin.com/in/harshpamnani/

Praise for Booming Brands, Volume 1

'Using journeys of remarkable Indian companies, Harsh Pamnani has written an interesting primer on brand building. A highly relevant read.' **Harsh Mariwala, Chairman, Marico**

'There are many "Made in India" brands that are getting noticed at the global stage, but their journeys are mostly unnoticed. Harsh has done a great job by bringing together these journeys in the form of referable case studies. Packed with a wealth of ideas and learnings from diverse businesses, this book is an essential handbook for anyone interested in understanding how to create an admirable brand from scratch.' **Ronnie Screwvala, Chairperson and Co-Founder, upGrad**

'Congratulations to Harsh Pamnani for the path-breaking book of Indian origin. The brands selected represent a good cross-section of both digital and brick-and-mortar situations. Harsh, for long, has been a prolific writer. His 50-plus articles reflect his creativity, imagination and deep insights. The title of the book is very apt and lessons shared by Harsh would make the readers rich in their knowledge and conceptual base. During the last 42 years of my association with MBA education, in India and abroad, I have always felt the acute deficit of intellectual capital rooted in India. Harsh's book has contributed greatly in filling this void. I wish the book grand success.' **Professor Sharad Sarin, (Retd) Professor, XLRI, Jamshedpur and author of *Business Management: Concepts and Cases* and *Strategic Brand Management for B2B Markets***

'In this well-researched book, Harsh Pamnani traces the journey from inception to taken-for-grantedness of a number of new and great "Made in India" brands, demystifying how brands such as Goli Vada Pav, Zomato and Shaadi.com have become compelling value propositions. A must-read book for seasoned marketing professionals as well as entrepreneurs.' **Anand Narasimhan, Shell Professor of Global Leadership and Dean of Research, IMD Switzerland**

'Congratulations, Harsh, on taking the initiative to chronicle the journey of these new-age companies, some of which have become household brands. Having seen the journey from close quarters for a few of them, I have always felt the need for these stories to be told more widely for other entrepreneurs to benefit from them and for others to get inspired. This book beautifully captures the backstory of many powerful domestic brands and is a must-read for those who want to learn from the experiences of some very successful next-generation business leaders.' **G.V. Ravishankar, Managing Director, Sequoia Capital, India**

'The mega-brands around us were built at a time, place and around people largely unfamiliar to most people. We just know and have a definite view about the product or service represented by that brand. Harsh Pamnani has in a way democratised the process of creating brands by incorporating them into stories and with people with whom everyday people can identify. Aspirational role models inspire us; attainable role models drive us to action. Harsh has provided us with a "can do" guide to brand creation.' **Sridar Iyengar, Chairman, ICICI Venture and former Chairman and CEO, KPMG, India**

'In the chronicles of the business and startup world, the entrepreneur is the heroine, at the centre of every conversation. Harsh has brilliantly shifted the focus to the brand, something that lasts far longer on the minds of consumers, something that deserves far more attention.' **Anand Lunia, Founding Partner, India Quotient**

'Harsh has provided some fascinating insights into homegrown brands in a large market like India. His hard work and passion in researching facts and identifying unique success factors is reflected in every page of the book. This book is particularly useful for those who want an "outside-in" perspective on building brands' **Vineet Malhotra, Entrepreneur, Startup Advisor, and former Managing Director, BlackRock, San Francisco**

'Building million-dollar brands requires nuance, dexterity and the ability to build cultural resonance. Harsh Pamnani has "cracked the code" for brand-building in arguably the world's most ascendant market—India. Replete with insight into those who have been there and done it, this book is a must for those aspiring to do so!' **David Bell, Professor, The Wharton School, University of Pennsylvania and Founding Partner, Idea Farm Ventures**

VOLUME 1

BOOMING BRANDS

INSPIRING JOURNEYS OF 11 'MADE IN INDIA' BRANDS

HARSH PAMNANI

First published in hardback by TV18 Broadcast Ltd in 2018

First published in paperback by Westland Business, an imprint of Westland Books, a division of Nasadiya Technologies Private Limited, in 2023

No. 269/2B, First Floor, 'Irai Arul', Vimalraj Street, Nethaji Nagar, Alapakkam Main Road, Maduravoyal, Chennai 600095

Westland, the Westland logo, Westland Business and the Westland Business logo are the trademarks of Nasadiya Technologies Private Limited, or its affiliates.

ISBN: 9789357766043
10 9 8 7 6 5 4 3 2 1

Typeset by Jojy Philip, New Delhi
Printed at Parksons Graphics Pvt. Ltd

To my father, Surendra Pamnani, for becoming my
first source of inspiration
To my mother, Kanchan Pamnani, for inspiring me
to dream big

In memory of
Late Dr Manohar Chandwani, IET-DAVV, Indore,
an excellent motivator and mentor

Contents

Introduction

Since childhood, I have been curious about why a few businesses grow and many struggle. I have seen a few schools, coaching classes, restaurants, FMCG brands, shops, companies, etc. becoming market leaders and have seen many shrinking and disappearing. I have noticed businesses spending millions of dollars and countless work hours on marketing campaigns, and many people ignoring these campaigns.

Earlier, consumers had a lot more time and fewer choices, and mass media was a powerful marketing channel. Today, the number of marketing channels have increased and consumers don't have the time to listen to marketing messages. The pace of change is increasing, and new technologies and business models are invading mature industries. Every day, new competitors and dozens of new products are introduced. Consumers are demanding more diversity and customisation than ever. All these trends are creating new challenges for entrepreneurs and marketers. But even amid all these challenges, a few entrepreneurs have been able to create powerful brands. I have been curious to know how they did it.

To satisfy my curiosity, I have made many unconventional career choices. One of them was to join TiE (The Indus Entrepreneurs). TiE gave me the opportunity to interact with numerous entrepreneurs ranging from those in the idea stage to those running multibillion dollar organisations. I listened to their failures, successes and challenges and created my own set of learnings. I realised that, for creating brands, the marketing problems faced by established businesses many years ago are troubling emerging businesses today too. Meanwhile, for sustaining their brands, established businesses are curious about the innovative marketing strategies of fast-growing startups.

I have also met many professionals, marketers and students who expressed that there is enough material available on the growth trajectories of international brands, but not enough about Indian brands. I felt that I could give some structure to my learnings and come up with referable material that could fill this void and be leveraged by the many people interested in learning from the journeys of today's rising brands.

I created my book-writing plan keeping my personal resources such as time and money in mind and then choosing booming brands in various niches. I defined the structure of the stories by covering the 'why', 'how' and 'what' of selected brands and their journeys. I pitched this plan to multiple brands. Fortunately, many of the founders liked my idea and agreed to give me their time. After many hectic days and sleepless nights, I was able to give shape to this book that covers winning lessons from 11 new-age and admirable brands of India.

There are many excellent books and case studies written by both international and Indian authors on the topics of marketing, brand management and entrepreneurs' journeys. The purpose of this book is not to become a substitute for, or a supplement to, any of the available materials. It is a passionate initiative to share learnings on brand-building along with the backstories of a few entrepreneurs who built something out of nothing.

Please note that this book contains brand journeys originally written between 2017 and 2018 and republished in 2023. While the stories are based on a particular timeline and do not reflect the latest developments in these brands' journeys and the lives of the individuals mentioned, the book provides valuable insights into how these new-age brands were created from scratch, how they achieved popularity in crowded and competitive markets, and how the entrepreneurs behind them identified new opportunities to develop million-dollar businesses. These timeless lessons from the hard-earned successes of these brands from multiple industries and domains can help you carve out your own journey and brand strategy.

Becoming a one-stop destination for all entertainment needs

Sometimes a big discovery or a brilliant business idea is triggered in a magical 'aha' moment. You are going about your everyday life when, unexpectedly, some inspiration or insight strikes you. Newton had such a moment when an apple fell on his head, Ray Kroc had it when he noticed the burger-making process of the McDonald brothers, and Dietrich Mateschitz had it when he discovered a jetlag-cure drink in Thailand. These 'aha' moments gave us the theory of gravity and brands like McDonald's and Red Bull.

In 1999, Ashish Hemrajani had a similar 'aha' moment while vacationing in South Africa. A radio commercial promoting ticket sales for rugby prompted him to think about organising the entertainment ticketing space in India.

Some businesses need more than one attempt before they become successful. So was the case with this business idea of Hemrajani's. After starting and shutting down a few ventures based on the idea he had, in 2007, Ashish and his team launched

BookMyShow. Today, BookMyShow is India's largest online entertainment ticketing platform, covering categories such as movies, plays, live events and sports. Apart from this, the company has extensive entertainment content on its platform and runs Jukebox, an audio entertainment service which allows you to stream and download the latest music and podcasts.

Within the first decade of its existence, the brand achieved phenomenal growth and, with over 25 million customers, became the leader in its category. The data spoke for its success: BookMyShow had over 100 million page views and over 10 million tickets were being booked through the platform every month. The company has a presence in over 650 towns and cities in India as well as operations in countries such as Sri Lanka and Indonesia.

THE BEGINNING OF THE JOURNEY

Up until the 1990s, people in India would queue up for hours for a movie ticket. There were times when they'd reach the ticketing counter only to see a 'houseful' sign. Or they'd find tickets being sold in black but couldn't afford to buy them. They'd simply have to miss a movie they were keen to watch.

In 1999, Ashish Hemrajani, then a young MBA graduate working with an advertising firm in Mumbai, was holidaying in South Africa when he heard a radio advertisement promoting rugby tickets. This sparked an idea in his head: he could replicate this model in India and solve the issues that hundreds of people in the country were facing due to the absence of an organised ticketing platform for movies, plays and other events. Ashish immediately sent the most expensive text message of his life, worth ₹186, to his boss and said he was quitting his job.

On his return to Mumbai the next day, Ashish started working on a business plan. In time, he co-founded India's first entertainment ticketing company, Go4ticketing.com, with his friends Parikshit Dar and Rajesh Balpande. Those were the days of the dotcom boom and soon, private equity firm Chase Capital Partners JP Morgan invested in the company and it became a sub-brand belonging to Hindustan Times' portal Go4i.com. Later, News Corp. bought the previous investor's stake and the company became Indya Tickets, a sub-brand of STAR Network's portal Indya.com.

The business growth, however, was short lived. By 2002, the dotcom bubble burst and Ashish's business was almost shut down. The period from 2002 to 2007 was a rough phase for the company, and it managed to survive by selling ticketing software and providing back-end ticketing services to cinema theatres. In 2007, seeing the growth of multiplexes, increased credit and debit card adoptions and internet penetration, Ashish and his team planned their comeback and launched BookMyShow. It took the market by storm and, over time, brought on board investors like Network18, Accel Partners, SAIF Partners and Stripes Group.

THE BRAND NAME: BOOKMYSHOW

BookMyShow is one of the most popular names among Indian internet brands. You might imagine that this iconic name was coined by some advertising or branding firm. The real story behind the name may come as a surprise.

In 2007, the company organised an internal contest to come up with a name for the new brand. In this contest, every participant was supposed to share three to five names meeting a few criteria, such as URL availability with a .com extension and others. The prize for the winner was an iPod touch.

Among those who participated in this contest was an intern in the engineering team. BookMyShow, one of the names he proposed, connected well with what the company did, and everybody liked it. This is a good example of how every person in the company can be important, and how small ideas can ultimately pay off in very big ways.

BUSINESS LESSONS

There are many important business lessons that can be learnt from the evolution of BookMyShow.

Focus on customers, not competitors

Many companies keep an eye on their competitors and try to follow their strategies. Watching the competition is good because it keeps you aware of the market conditions, but being obsessed with your competitors is not a great formula as it limits your mindset. Rather, if you focus on customers, you can come up with new ideas to wow them.

In 1999, Ashish had started his first venture with a focus on customers who wanted to watch movies and attend events but didn't have a hassle-free ticketing option. Establishing this concept in India was no child's play. During this period, the Indian market was not ready for internet-based businesses, payment gateways were not available and credit card usage was almost negligible. Also, within a short span of time, twenty-one competitors had emerged, and the market had become highly competitive. Rather than worrying too much about the competition, Ashish and his team focused on enhancing customer experience.

Selling tickets may look like a business of selling commoditised products as customers don't need to look at and feel the product before buying it. But it's actually a business of providing differentiable service. The experience of buying a product is a key differentiator and BookMyShow focused on improving its service to delight its customers.

In its early years, the company would buy a fixed amount of ticket inventory and sell it to customers through its fifteen call centres. To add further value and provide reliable options, these call centres were operational 24x7 and had easy dial-in numbers. As customers were not able to pay online or in advance, the company had staff to hand over tickets on a cash-on-delivery (COD) basis. Ashish focused on getting his team trained in every aspect of customer service from greeting customers when they called, to branding ticket envelopes, to even getting ready before delivering tickets to them. For example, the ticket delivery boy would remove his helmet, comb his hair, wear the company cap and tabard, and then meet the customer. Nowadays, these things look normal, but in the early 2000s they were not, and these became differentiating factors for the company.

Over a period, the company has done many other innovative things to keep itself ahead of the competition and make its customers comfortable. For instance, in the case of cancellation of a show by a movie theatre, the company immediately refunds the amount to its customers. The company has kept up with the evolution of technology and has moved from manual processes to automated ticketing processes at cinemas and multiplexes. It has set up automated ticket-collecting machines at select cinema houses. As in the case of self-check-in kiosks at airports, customers can simply place their debit or credit cards on the machine, which scans the card and prints the tickets.

The next level of growth for the company happened when it went online and started providing innovative solutions through its website and app, which have been recognised as being extremely user friendly. BookMyShow was the first website to simplify the ticket booking process. Interestingly, it doesn't require a customer to sign in. Instead of signing in first and then moving ahead for the transaction, a customer can go through the regular ticketing flow of selecting a movie, theatre, show and seat of choice; proceed to the payments page and then confirm their details by providing an email ID and a mobile number. The email ID and mobile number information recorded at the end are used for confirming the transaction and sending the ticket. The BookMyShow app was praised as one of the best apps of 2017 on both Google Play Store and Apple App Store, and it has crossed 50 million downloads.

Ashish says, 'Customers are evolving faster than ever before, if you don't evolve your business to match their speed, they will leave you.' Keeping in mind this philosophy, BookMyShow became the first Indian online ticketing brand to participate in the WhatsApp business pilot. As a part of this test, BookMyShow made WhatsApp a default ticket confirmation channel for all its users.

To enable individuals to choose the films that play in their local cinemas, BookMyShow has joined hands with India's largest movie distributor PVR Pictures for Vkaao, a web platform by PVR. As part of the partnership, BookMyShow makes use of its analytical capabilities to identify the right set of viewers and curate screenings while PVR focuses on the availability of a variety of films across genres and languages.

In 2016, due to its continued focus on improving customer experience, BookMyShow won the award for the best Omni-channel Customer Experience Brand.

Brand building is a marathon, not a sprint

A sprint is a full speed short-distance run whereas a marathon is a long-distance race, which needs more stamina. Many people think that successful brands can be created quickly, which is a myth. Brands are built on a foundation of long-term focus, patience and perseverance. Steve Jobs once said, 'If you really look closely, most overnight successes took a long time.'

In 1999, when Big Tree Entertainment, the parent company of BookMyShow, began its operations, there was hardly any ecosystem in India to run digital businesses. Along with building the business, the team also focused on building the ecosystem. To serve the demand side, it ran the business through call centres and ticket delivery boys. To create the supply side, it installed ticketing software at theatres, provided them call centre services and helped them in selling their unsold inventory and increasing footfall. This was the time of the traditionally run single-screen theatres where systems were not automated and there were issues with internet connectivity. To book the inventory, the company would block seats by paying in advance and then would sell booked tickets to interested customers. This was not a cost-efficient model as the company ended up with unsold tickets on weekdays while running short on weekends.

In its initial years, the company grew, but the revenue came at extensive cost. Then, in 2002, the dot-com bubble burst led to the collapse of the business model. The company went from 150 people to just 6 people, and moved from a 2,500 square feet office to a 138 square feet apartment in Bandra. Till 2007, the company managed to survive by selling ticketing software and providing back-end ticketing services to cinema theatres. This was the period when the multiplex sector started growing and the company turned into a call centre for multiplexes such as PVR and Cinemax, among others.

By 2007, the internet had become more prevalent in India, and Ashish and his team launched a tech-savvy and cost-efficient business by the name of BookMyShow—India's first online entertainment ticketing aggregator. The company started increasing its ticket inventory for all popular film genres, including drama, action, comedy, romance and thriller. Along with Hindi and English cinema, it started increasing its base to regional cinema such as Gujarati, Marathi, Malayalam, Tamil and Telugu. Over time, the company expanded its base to non-movie entertainment spaces as well. It started moving from top-tier cities to small towns and expanded its operations to many international locations. Ashish says, 'When an American brand comes to countries like India, people look up to it as an aspiration. That's not the case when an Indian brand goes international. Building the brand in every new geography is a new effort from scratch.'

Though initially, the company's focus had been only on ticket bookings, to keep its audience engaged and provide them with anything and everything related to entertainment in one place, the company continuously updates its platform with content like trailers, ratings, reviews and offers. It has also launched Jukebox, an audio entertainment service that is becoming the one-stop destination for music lovers. It serves an extensive database of both Indian and international music, as well as other non-music audio content comprising talk shows and genre-based podcasts. Ashish says, 'To keep enjoying a marathon and avoiding burnout, one should maintain a work-life balance and look forward to Friday evenings, in the same way they look forward to Monday mornings.'

Impacting the lives of people around you

Herb Kelleher once said, 'Your employees come first. And if you treat your employees right, guess what? Your customers come back, and that makes your shareholders happy. Start with employees and the rest follows from that.'

In addition to conventional business metrics, Ashish gives a lot of importance to the metrics of employee care. The company believes in contributing towards the development of its employees and runs several initiatives towards this end, such as Vedanta classes, yoga sessions and leadership talks. Additionally, it has several people-friendly practices, among which is a voluntary fund for employees that comes in handy when someone within the organisation needs financial help. The company also runs a mediclaim programme for employees, which covers their spouse, two children and parents, with no co-pay.

Then there is the company's food programme, wherein employees above a certain designation pay a premium for the food that is served in the office. People below a certain salary pay 50 to 60 per cent of that value, while all office boys, peons and outsourced staff pay only ₹20 for the same food. Everyone eats in the same cafeteria. Similarly, there are no separate executive and office toilets.

There have been a few interesting outcomes of the people development initiatives at the company. For example, the head of the contact centre team at BookMyShow had joined the company as a representative many years ago. Over the years, she became a team leader, then a supervisor, and today, she leads a team of 270 people. Similarly, the head of warehouse operations had started out as an office boy. The company paid for the education of its maid's daughter and then gave her a job opportunity in its call centre. As another remarkable initiative, the company funds the part-time education of some of its junior staff, like office boys, who aspire to study and grow.

Following a similar thought, of positively impacting society, the company runs a charity initiative called BookASmile.

Through this initiative, the company works towards enriching the lives of the less fortunate with entertainment-led experiences in the areas of sports, culture, music, art, movies and so on. For this charitable initiative, the company collects funds by allowing customers to donate from ₹1 to ₹5 with every transaction.

The collected amount is utilised for interesting programmes. For example, in 2016, BookASmile organised a special screening of the movie *Sultan* starring Salman Khan. The actor came to greet the 1,200 kids who were part of the event. Along with online crowdfunding platform Ketto, BookASmile organised the biggest ever online fundraising event 'Book 6 Million Smiles' for NGOs in India and contributed ₹60 lakhs in funding.

In 2017, the organisation ran an initiative to bring filmmaking to the grassroots. Along with multiple NGOs, the organisation brought together filmmakers like Kabir Bedi, Satish Kaushik, Prakash Jha, Farah Khan and Jackie Shroff to Himachal Pradesh, Maharashtra, Odisha and Bihar, and taught the various aspects of filmmaking to over 250 children. These children, who were between the ages of 4 and 16 years, made 12 short films, which were showcased at the Alive Short Film Festival.

Along with many other initiatives, BookASmile supported a few girls from Jharkhand to play soccer, and it took a few students to SECMOL, an alternative school in Ladakh that exposes students to real-life skills and empowers them to chart their own course.

Understand what creates the marketability of your product

Marketability refers to the attractiveness or appeal of an idea, product or service. There are various drivers that facilitate marketability, such as brand trust, friction-less transaction, packaging, taste, distribution, price and quality. Different drivers of marketability work during different stages of business, in different markets and in different cultures.

Ashish says, 'If you keep on doing the same thing better, you might become efficient in that thing. But your competitors will keep on doing new things and your customers' expectations will keep on evolving. Keep pushing the envelope, try new things to improve marketability of your product.'

Earlier, when the business was new and customers had not tried the product, BookMyShow ran discounts to build a critical mass. But in the long run, giving discounts is not a viable strategy because a fine balance between price and quality must be maintained. The company has continuously worked to improve the product from multiple dimensions, such as search functionality, buying experience, friction-less payment processes and so on. It has added many new features on its platform; relevant content, pre-booking concessions, food coupons and split costs, to name a few.

Another dimension of marketability is variety. BookMyShow has been continuously increasing the breadth and depth of entertainment options for its customers. It has listings of almost all major events, plays and sports in every major city and at multiple timings. It is a one-stop destination for live events. Annually, it sells tickets of over 1,000 events, including Sunburn, Sula Wine Fest, Auto Expo and many others. Tickets of Ed Sheeran Live in Mumbai were sold out on BookMyShow in just 48 minutes. BookMyShow has partnered with all major Indian production houses and studios with real-time ticketing for major cinema chains like Inox, PVR, Big Cinemas, Cinemax and Fun Cinemas. For the mega blockbuster *Baahubali 2*, BookMyShow alone sold over 16 million tickets.

Over time, its partnerships have become the drivers of marketability. BookMyShow has partnered with all major banks and payment gateways that keep on running offers for their customers on transactions made through its platform. Additionally, BookMyShow Corporate Solutions, the B2B wing of the company, partners with corporates for their customised entertainment voucher requirements for promotional activities, employee rewards, lead generation and other incentives.

One more dimension of marketability is customers' evangelism. In 2017, the company introduced its first-ever benefits programme, BookMyShow Superstars, as part of which it identifies a base of its most loyal customers and offers them a wide variety of rewards and benefits such as gift vouchers, free movie seat upgrades, access to exclusive premier invitations for movies and so on. For the Road to Ultra concert featuring The Chainsmokers, a few winners were chosen from BookMyShow Superstars. The winners got a once-in-a-lifetime opportunity to fly to the concert in an air-conditioned BookMyShow branded chopper from Pawan Hans, Juhu to Mahalaxmi Race Course in Mumbai. They received red carpet treatment and were accompanied by one of the artists performing at the concert. This programme not only created PR buzz for the brand but also turned many customers into brand ambassadors and evangelists.

Think differently about technology

A lot of people differentiate between brick-and-mortar and digital businesses. This is not a correct way of differentiating, as almost all businesses are people businesses and involve emotions and physical infrastructure. For instance, if you look at BookMyShow, it can be called a digital business because the customer interacts with the platform through a mobile app and website. But all cinemas, events, plays, etc. are running in physical environments and people watch them in physical environments, that is, in buildings made of brick and mortar.

Similarly, you may consider Uber a digital business because it operates through a mobile app, but it is solving a transportation problem in the physical world. It connects a customer with a driver in the physical world, and the customer takes the ride in a physical environment.

On the other hand, even if a business looks to be an out-and-out brick-and-mortar business at first glance, such as hotels, they need a strong layer of technology at the back-end to run efficiently. All businesses, whether they look like digital or brick-and-mortar from the outside, need to have a technological layer of data, analytics, machine learning, business intelligence and other upcoming technologies to make data-driven decisions, understand consumer behaviour and solve their business problems quickly and efficiently.

Ashish says, 'Today, every business needs to be a tech-driven business. Any business that is not using technology is going to suffer or sink.' In its previous avatar, the company sold tickets through a call centre and delivered physical tickets through delivery boys. Also, for blocking seats, it had to purchase tickets in advance. This was a highly cost-intensive model. In its new avatar, the company delivers e-tickets on mobile and email. In this model, the increased demand is managed by technology in a cost-efficient way. Moreover, advancements like automation of processes at theatres have made information available in real time, so customers can directly buy tickets using online payment channels.

Ashish says, 'A business will die, if it doesn't have data analytics. For any business to forecast and take decisions, data analytics is really the heart of business.' BookMyShow uses data analytics and machine learning technologies to understand its overall market share and identify the revenue potential not only on a geographical basis, but also for specific show times and venues.

It collects vast information about customer sales, timing of new releases, movie genres, actors, theatre locations, theatre sizes and more. It also understands the profiles of customers attending various events.

To enable its transformation into a content-driven entertainment destination, the company has been working on a big data project wherein it is organising all the unorganised data on the film industry, such as cast, crew, film actors and so on.

Moreover, it continuously works on new ideas to surprise its customers with wonderful experiences. For instance, the company has developed an in-house personalisation engine which runs predictive algorithms on user data. It predicts which customer would like to watch which movie based on their past selections. Built on predictive analytics, a major part of the platform is customised for the specific user and they get recommendations that are most relevant to them.

Technology has also helped the business build a reach and target the right audience. Earlier, when the company would advertise through newspapers and hoardings, the reach of the business was limited and, due to lack of control on the target audience, spillage was high. But digital channels have helped the company target the right audience having the right set of characteristics. For instance, the audience can be targeted based on criteria such as: interested in movies, wants to go out and watch, has internet connection, has credit card, has an ability to pay for the ticket and so on.

ASHISH HEMRAJANI
TICKET
ADMIT ONE
4672698
ENTERTAINMENT
SHOWTIME
TICKET

Dietrich Mateschitz once said, 'If we don't create the market, it doesn't exist.' Ashish's journey is a testament to this statement. He created a new market not by inventing a new product but by inventively selling an ordinary one. The amazing journey of a company, from an idea to one of the largest e-commerce platforms in the country, is nothing less than a movie story. This story has a rise, a downfall and then a spectacular comeback to fame. It has a villain in the form of the unorganised entertainment market and a reincarnated hero in the form of BookMyShow.

Advice from Ashish Hemrajani

- More companies die of indigestion than of starvation. If you have capital, use it frugally rather than burning it inefficiently.
- Rather than worrying too much about external factors, focus on the things that are in your control. Don't complain about the environment, just keep changing and adapting.
- The role of marketing is to create new users, more users, loyal users and lifetime users. Whatever a business needs to do to get these users is marketing's job.

JAYAASHREE INDUSTRIES

A powerhouse of local FMCG brands

What do you think is required to create great brands from the bottom of the pyramid? Exposure to rural marketing, degrees from world-class institutions, experience at global multinationals, pots of money, or something else? To know what it really takes, you can explore the journey of Arunachalam Muruganantham, a school dropout from a small village near Coimbatore. His humble background as a workshop worker and lack of external funding did not stop him from revolutionising menstrual hygiene for women at the bottom of the pyramid.

Arunachalam is credited with inventing the world's first low-cost sanitary-pad-making machine branded as Jayaashree. This machine can manufacture sanitary pads for less than a third of the cost of commercial pads. In 2009, Arunachalam received the President's award for the best technical invention. In 2014, *TIME* magazine named him amongst the 100 Most Influential People in the World. In 2016, he was awarded the Padma Shri, one of the highest civilian awards, by the Government of India. He has received many other prestigious national and international awards, including Inspired Leadership Award from The Performance Theatre in 2016. Moreover, the Hindi movie *Pad Man*, starring Akshay Kumar, is a biopic on Arunachalam.

Arunachalam's machines have been installed in almost all the Indian states and around twenty-five other countries. Today, using these machines, women in many villages have created more than 1,000 local brands of sanitary napkins, and are able to earn sustainable livelihoods and live with dignity.

THE SCALE OF THE PROBLEM SOLVED BY ARUNACHALAM

So, what's different between men and women? They breathe, eat, drink and sleep alike. But unlike men, women go through a monthly hormonal process known as menstruation or a period. The average age of menarche (the onset of menstruation in adolescents) is twelve years and each menstruation period usually lasts for an average of five days. In this process, blood and mucosal tissue gets discharged from the inner lining of the uterus through the vagina. During this period, women need absorbent material, like a sanitary pad, to absorb and retain menstrual fluid discharge, prevent leaks and stay comfortable. You would have seen advertisements of disposable sanitary pads such as Procter & Gamble's Whisper, Johnson & Johnson's Stayfree and Kimberly Clark's Kotex and may have thought that if there is a problem, MNCs have provided the required solution.

But there is a catch. Many women are not able to use sanitary pads due to lack of awareness and because the mainstream ones are unaffordable.

Let's look at the problem of affordability. Nearly half of the world's population, that is, more than 3 billion people live on less than $2.50 a day. By far, India has the largest number of poor people in the world. Women in this segment can't afford to regularly purchase high-cost sanitary pads manufactured by international brands. During their menstrual cycle, these women often end up using a variety of absorbent materials, such as unhygienic pieces of cloth, to collect the menstrual blood. As a result, they risk contracting many infectious diseases.

Now let's look at the problem of awareness. Most of the time, women don't feel comfortable talking about menstruation with men. There are still many social taboos around menstruation, especially in rural India. Women are even considered untouchable during this period—they can't visit temples or public places, they're not allowed to cook or touch the water supply and so on. There are also myths and fears, such as women who use pads will go blind or that if an unmarried girl uses a sanitary pad and a dog gets access to the used pad, the girl will not get married or a family member will die, and so on.

Due to a lack of awareness and the issue of affordability, women use old pieces of cloth and other unhygienic substances such as sand, sawdust, leaves and even ash. As per a Nielson report, only 12 per cent of Indian women use sanitary napkins. Arunachalam shared, 'This number further dips to 2 per cent in rural India.'

It is saddening that approximately 70 per cent of all reproductive diseases in India are caused by poor menstrual hygiene, which can also affect maternal mortality. Besides health problems, it can also have an adverse impact on the right of education of girls as many of them end up dropping out of school.

ARUNACHALAM'S MISSION: THE BEGINNING

In 1998, Arunachalam got married to Shanthi. Once, he discovered his wife carrying a dirty ragged cloth with blood on it. It reminded him of the cloth his sisters would use. Innocently, he asked his wife if she had hurt herself. She replied that she was going through her monthly menstruation cycle. He asked her why she didn't use proper sanitary pads which were available at local stores. Shanthi replied that the pads were too expensive, and if she bought those pads there would be no money left to buy milk for the family.

Wanting to impress his wife, Arunachalam went into town to buy a sanitary pad for her. The shopkeeper handed it to him hurriedly, as if he was buying contraband. He weighed the pad in his hand and wondered why a pad with approximately 10 g of cotton, which at the time cost 10 paisa, should be sold for ₹4, which amounted to 40 times the price of the raw material. He decided he could make cheaper pads himself.

EXPERIMENTATION AND CHALLENGES

Arunachalam designed an experimental pad using cotton and gave it to his wife for testing. She told him it was the worst napkin that she had ever used. Arunachalam repeatedly made prototypes, took feedback, made changes, and came up with new versions of his sanitary pad.

To test his prototypes and get feedback, he had to wait for his wife's monthly cycle. To avoid the month-long delay in testing his pads, he decided to ask his sisters to try them out as well. After a few trials, his wife and sisters stopped cooperating. He started looking for volunteers who could test his pads, but most were too shy to discuss their menstrual issues with him or provide concrete feedback. Later, he distributed his pads to girls in the local medical college and asked them to return the pads after use. He managed to convince twenty students to try out his pads, but it still didn't work out as he found out that the feedback was not genuine with three girls trying to fill in the feedback of twenty.

It was very difficult to get women to try his sanitary pads, so he decided to test the pads on himself. He started wearing pads and, using a football bladder filled with animal blood, he started testing the effectiveness of his prototypes.

DISCOURAGEMENT AND OPPOSITION

His wife couldn't bear his obsession for pads. She misunderstood his interactions with other women and left home. When his mother saw him storing a bunch of used sanitary napkins in their home, she too misunderstood him and left. Everyone thought he had gone mad. When his fellow villagers saw him washing his bloodstained undergarments, they jumped to the conclusion that he was suffering from a sexual disease. He became a subject of ridicule in his village, and the villagers were convinced that he was possessed by evil spirits. They decided to chain him upside down to a tree so that he could be healed by a local healer. Eventually, he left the village.

BECOMING A SOLUTION PROVIDER

After struggling for more than two years, Arunachalam finally discovered that commercial pads used cellulose fibres derived from the pulp of the bark of the pine tree. The fibres helped the pads absorb menstrual discharge while retaining their shape. But what shook him was the discovery that the imported machines that made the pads from this material cost around ₹3.5 crore. He took up the monumental challenge of building a cheaper machine and after persisting for four-and-a-half years, he succeeded in creating one that cost around ₹65,000. He sourced the processed pinewood pulp from a supplier in the USA and used his machine to grind, de-fibrate, press and sterilise the pads with ultraviolet radiation before packaging them for sale.

In 2006, he participated in a contest at IIT Madras and showcased his prototype. He won first prize (out of 943 entries) in the contest. With the financial assistance of ₹15 lakh from IIT Madras and National Innovation Foundation, Ahmedabad, he started his sanitary napkin manufacturing unit in Coimbatore.

BIRTH OF THE BRAND NAME: JAYAASHREE

Arunachalam named his manufacturing unit Jayaashree Industries. It is a firm that manufacturers and markets these machines to rural women across India and several other countries. He named his machine after his niece, Jayaashree. There is an interesting story behind this brand name. Even when Arunachalam was ostracised by his community and family, his sister would give him food. Since he was not allowed to enter her house, she would throw the food out from the window for him to catch. Later, his sister gave birth to a daughter and Arunachalam named his invention after his niece.

BUSINESS LESSONS

There are many important business lessons that can be learnt from the evolution of the brand Jayaashree. A few of them are as follows.

Focus on market creation over market sharing

In the market-sharing approach, entrepreneurs identify an established market, look at the business models of dozens of existing players and try to gain market share by coming up with a similar offering. Most of the times, they forget that to gain a bigger market share they need to win over their competitors' market shares. They invest money in advertising, discounts and distribution, but later realise that the player with better financial resources will not allow them to win the game. On the other hand, in the market-creation approach, entrepreneurs identify unexplored problems, come up with new solutions, educate the market and create new standards.

When big companies were focusing on market segments that could afford expensive sanitary pads and were busy winning over each other's market share, Arunachalam looked at the market segment at the bottom of the pyramid that was not getting addressed by global brands. When bigger companies were positioning their products around comfort, Arunachalam talked about hygiene, a subject no one spoke about earlier.

When Arunachalam adopted the market-creation approach, he neither had case studies nor proven business models to refer to. But he persisted and continued in his exploration. Eventually, he created a huge opportunity not only for himself but also for millions of poor women.

Collect not only quantitative feedback but also qualitative feedback

Marketers love numbers, that is, quantitative information. They use past numbers, global numbers, competitors' numbers, statistical surveys and so on, to predict their future strategy. In established markets, numbers are useful to understand business performance. In emerging markets, numbers don't reflect what's happening in the human mind, especially when business models and products are yet to be proven. A qualitative approach gives an opportunity to understand customers' needs at a human level, analyse their attitude, empathise with them and build relationships.

Arunachalam constantly collected feedback on his sanitary pads from women. Initially, he created a non-branded sanitary napkin and later, he created a brand called Covai. He was aware that medical stores and departmental stores are male-dominated places and women don't feel comfortable buying sanitary pads from men. He also understood that keeping his brand at a store would require credits to retailers, transportation costs and a sum running in crores to make his brand available at thousands of retail stores in Coimbatore. With this insight he created his own door-to-door delivery model and started supplying to women directly as per their requirement.

He also realised that in categories like sanitary pads, low-cost products don't work, as people equate low cost with low quality. On the other hand, if a brand with proper packaging is sold at the same price as that of established brands or higher, then it is positively perceived. Over a period, he started getting positive feedback on his sanitary pads and gained the confidence to present his innovation at IIT Madras.

Innovate your business model

In any industry, there is always a possibility of innovating the business model. Business areas such as processes, manufacturing, distribution, engagement with customers and suppliers, resource management, etc. have scope for innovations. The challenger who identifies the innovation opportunities in a business model can disrupt the industry.

Arunachalam observed that though global brands have been around for decades, have sufficient resources and have spent a lot of money on advertisements, the usage of sanitary pads has been very low. He started exploring the causes of low usage of pads and realised that there are a few unmet needs present in the market. First, women in every country, state, region and area have different menstrual cycles and sanitary pad requirements, but global brands manufacture and package almost similar kind of pads for women everywhere. Second, India has over 1,000 vernacular languages, but global brands package and market their products mostly in English. Third, retail models such as departmental stores and medical stores are male-dominated and women are not comfortable conversing with men about menstruation and sanitary pads. Fourth, retailing is an expensive model. To sell any products through retailers, brands, especially new ones, need to keep a few packs at every store and wait for payment till those few packs are sold. Imagine the amount of investment required, if five packs need to be kept at thousands of retail stores. The cost of transportation, including hiring drivers, needs to be taken into account.

With his mindset to challenge the status quo, Arunachalam created a new business model—'Detailing'.

He explained, 'Unlike global companies' business models that have centralised production, distribution overheads and then dependency on retailers, Detailing decentralises production across multiple villages.' He added, 'It is a very cost-effective business model as it doesn't have the overhead of transportation. Additionally, it doesn't have middlemen such as dealers, distributors and retailers, so their profit margins are saved.' Arunachalam pointed out that their products do not need to be advertised through TV or newspapers, as word of mouth among women is a powerful marketing channel.

In this model, Jayaashree Industries provides machines to women self-help groups, NGOs, women entrepreneurs and female students. It also provides in-depth training to operate

Figure: Workflow of the 'Detailing' business model

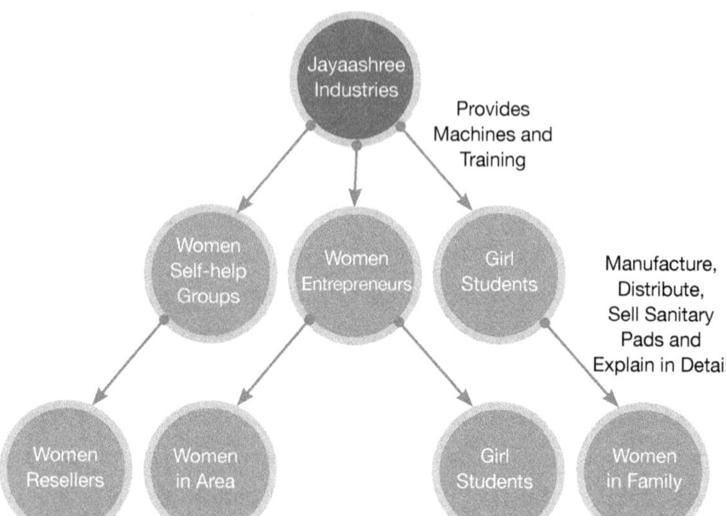

these machines along with educating young women on menstruation. Sometimes machines are given for free till women start earning money by selling pads. Arunachalam funds these machines through his personal savings or through support from corporate CSR initiatives. When women start making money by manufacturing and selling sanitary pads, they are assisted in acquiring loans from banks and government schemes. Sometimes machines are even given through barter system in exchange for buffalos, cows and goats. Using these machines, women make affordable sanitary pads and sell them to other women in the village while imparting training on the importance of hygiene and the use of sanitary pads.

Machines are demonstrated in weekly village markets. Women from nearby areas watch other women create sanitary pads using the machines and then try to follow the same process in their own villages. Women in various regions have created their own brands and today Jayaashree Industries has a portfolio of around 1,000 brands which are created, packaged and marketed in vernacular languages by women in their respective areas. In case women don't have the money to buy sanitary pads, they exchange pads for onions and potatoes through the barter system. Girls who would earlier skip school or college during their periods are now able to attend their classes. They manufacture their own sanitary pads, sell pads in their sphere of influence, and educate their mothers and grandmothers on the importance of hygiene during menstruation. Detailing has become a model of sustainable livelihood for women.

Another interesting aspect of this model is that it's a woman-to-woman model. Women trust the word-of-mouth of other women much more than any number of advertisements. In this model, a woman can go to any other woman and ask even basic questions related to menstruation and hygiene. Additionally, when women see other women using sanitary pads, they feel empowered to ignore social taboos and take care of their health and hygiene.

Arunachalam has also aligned his organisational structure to meet the needs of this business. He hit upon the idea of a circular management model, which he prefers over the hierarchal top-down structure. In a top-down hierarchical model, sometimes human ego comes in the way and the people at the top become disconnected with the people at the bottom. Here, the main driver of motivation for people is to get promoted to the next level. But in the circular management model, anyone can interact with anyone without any ego and hierarchy. Also, if Arunachalam or anyone else, including a woman entrepreneur operating a machine, is not available, information and workflow doesn't stop; the next person in the circle can be contacted to take things ahead. This model is very much applicable in the context of social entrepreneurship, as the motivation for people is not to get promoted to the next level, but to support and promote a social cause.

Create a great product and test it in tough markets

If a product is bad, no amount of advertising can make it look good. Many marketers perceive that strong media campaigns can hide deficiencies in the product and customer relationships. But the reality is that a brand must first establish itself in the marketplace and only then can it get genuine media coverage.

Arunachalam created an initial version of his machine using wood. This version had basic features required to create sanitary pads. Though he won the first prize at IIT Madras for his invention, judges had doubts about the feasibility of his business model. Usually, people prefer to choose easy markets to test their business models, but Arunachalam did just the opposite. Instead of testing it in his own state of Tamil Nadu, which is considered a developed state, he chose Bihar, one of the poorest and most underdeveloped states in India. His approach was, if he could crack his model in Bihar, he could make it work anywhere. After testing his model in Bihar, he tested it in other equally challenging states, such as Madhya Pradesh, Rajasthan and Uttar Pradesh. Learnings from these tough markets helped him in improving both his product and business model.

Through his pilots, he kept on simplifying the machine and made it more efficient and effective. For field trials, Arunachalam himself goes to the most risky and underdeveloped areas where he needs to convince the village head (sarpanch) and other men to allow him to talk with women about menstruation and menstrual hygiene. In the less risky villages, he sends his experienced team members and in the least risky suburban areas, he sends his junior team members.

Today, Arunachalam enjoys a lot of media coverage and publicity for his work, because he has spent close to a decade in establishing his product and its usage in rural markets.

Use storytelling to build strong brands

Storytelling is not only an art but also the best marketing technique. Stories have the power to spread ideas from person to person. Moreover, social media such as YouTube, Facebook and Twitter amplify these stories.

With his own story, Arunachalam has won the hearts of millions. Though today Arunachalam is a well-renowned speaker with millions of fans, his journey has not been easy. He realised that to spread his idea he had to communicate not only in local languages with rural women, but also in English with business, academic and social leaders globally.

In his first attempt at communicating his ideas, at TiE Bangalore, Arunachalam spoke in Tamil and an interpreter translated his speech into English. The interpreter, however, couldn't convey Arunachalam's passion and journey in an effective way to the audience. To avoid depending on an interpreter, Arunachalam gave his next talk in broken English. This talk at the TiE Summit in 2009, Asia's largest entrepreneurship conference then, organised by TiE Mumbai, received a standing ovation from a crowd of over 2,000 people.

From then onwards, Arunachalam has given lectures at many reputed platforms, including prestigious Indian institutes such as IITs, IIMs as well as international institutes like Harvard. His TED talk has been viewed more than a million times and his INK talk has more than 7,00,000 views. His story was the subject of a prize-winning documentary *Menstrual Man*. Additionally, Akshay Kumar's movie *Pad Man* is a biopic on Arunachalam. In the recent past, Arunachalam was on a panel with Bill Gates, and he has also been invited as a speaker for corporate events led by leaders such as the Future Group CEO Kishore Biyani and Unilever CEO Paul Polman.

Arunachalam's story and his powerful delivery style have created a lot of awareness about menstrual hygiene globally and have gained attention and advocacy for the cause.

Balance fame and responsibility

Fame is the state of being known by many people as a celebrity. It is difficult to attain fame and even more so to remain grounded after attaining it. Arunachalam has received many accolades and awards for his commendable work on educating women on menstruation, invention of a low-cost sanitary-pad-making-machine, innovative business model and, most importantly, for empowering poor women to live a dignified life through hygiene and a stable livelihood.

Over time, Arunachalam's life has become like a pendulum. He is constantly swaying between a luxurious lifestyle while travelling for international conferences and extreme hardships while travelling to risky, remote areas to fulfill his responsibilities.

Usually, a business leader's fame helps in influencing his customers and driving business growth. But in the case of Arunachalam, his customers hardly understand the meaning of the recognition he has received in prestigious forums. Though he is recognised in influential circles, which is helpful in gathering support for his cause, he is still largely unknown amongst his rural customers.

> **The Impact of Jayaashree**
> Today, each of Arunachalam's machines provides employment to ten women and converts around 3,000 women to sanitary pad users. Women can produce 200–1,000 pads a day, which

ARUNACHALAM MURUGANANTHAM

SANITARY PAD

sell for an average of about ₹2.5 each. Women choose their own brand name for the sanitary pads they produce. Jayaashree the machine has helped create thousands of brands by the women and for the women. Arunachalam's aim is to create millions of jobs for poor women worldwide. As of now, only around 10 per cent of menstruating women in India use sanitary pads. Arunachalam's mission is to take this number to 100 per cent. Furthermore, he has plans to expand his machine's impact to 106 countries across the globe, including Kenya, Nigeria, Mauritius, the Philippines and Bangladesh.

To extend his innovation further, Arunachalam is working on a low-cost sanitary-pad-making machine that can operate without electricity, as the unavailability of electricity continues to be a major problem in many rural areas of India.

Advice from Arunachalam Muruganantham

- Don't be in a hurry to become a billionaire, try to solve a problem first.
- Domain knowledge is important for building a product. If you are an expert in business, collaborate with someone who is an expert in a particular domain.
- Don't try to become Abhimanyu. Though Abhimanyu was one of the greatest warriors in the Mahabharata, he had limited knowledge of warfare. He was only able to enter the Chakravyuha, but not able to come out of it. Many entrepreneurs plan to build startups without gaining the necessary expertise. They work for some time in a company, get fascinated by media stories of a few successful entrepreneurs, assume that ideas copied from other countries would work in India and take the plunge. Like entering a Chakravyuha, starting an enterprise is one aspect. But like getting out of the Chakravyuha, making an enterprise successful needs expertise.

Marrying tradition with technology

Some of the biggest innovations are a result of someone trying to come up with a simplified solution for a complex problem affecting a large number of people. Using the power of the internet, innovative global brands like Google, Facebook and Amazon have simplified search, networking and shopping for the general public. Closer home, a global brand of Indian origin Shaadi.com has also solved one of the biggest problems in everyone's life—finding a suitable life partner.

Till some years ago, most Indians would look for a spouse within the limited scope of their extended family, circle of friends, neighbours and colleagues, or someone they met at social gatherings, in community networks, or from within the limited database of traditional matchmakers. However, with the advent of the internet, it has become possible to connect with people from across the globe, whom we may not have met otherwise. Shaadi.com realised this and brought profiles of people from all castes, communities, regions and professions to one place. It made the search for a life partner simpler, quicker and broader.

Started as an experiment in the year 1997, Shaadi.com is the world's largest matchmaking service company with a presence in international markets such as the USA, UK, Middle East and many more. Till now, more than 5 million marriages have been facilitated via connections through Shaadi.com.

During its journey, the company has won numerous awards and recognitions, such as: one of the top 50 most innovative companies in the world by Fast Company, the top 10 most visited websites in India by Alexa, the top 10 marketers in India by Business Today and the No. 1 matrimonial brand amongst digital brands in the 'Most Trusted Brands Survey' released by Brand Equity (Economic Times) in collaboration with AC Nielsen and many others.

This chapter covers the inspiring journey of Shaadi.com, one of the oldest and most popular Indian internet brands.

THE BEGINNING OF THE JOURNEY

In the mid-1990s, Anupam Mittal, the founder of Shaadi.com, was working in the USA. This was the period of the internet boom, and many online companies like Amazon and Yahoo were evolving, and companies like Netscape had gone public with multibillion dollar IPOs. Being a part of the ecosystem, he had seen how the internet was transforming businesses and impacting the lives of consumers.

In 1997, when Anupam came to India on a vacation, his father introduced him to a traditional matchmaker. The matchmaker would travel door to door carrying a briefcase that had biodatas of prospective brides and grooms. A conversation with the traditional matchmaker made Anupam realise that the choices of a prospective spouse available to him was limited to the size of the matchmaker's briefcase. Anupam figured that this limitation of profiles was not only a problem for him but for anyone looking to get married.

Because of his exposure to online businesses in the US, he quickly realised that he could solve this problem through the internet. He hired a small team in India to run the website, which he named Sagai.com. He monitored the progress of this experiment from the US.

BIRTH OF THE BRAND NAME: SHAADI.COM

In 2001, Anupam planned to turn his experiment into a full-time entrepreneurial venture. He quit his job in the US and moved back to India.

Shaadi is the Hindi word for matrimony. Every Indian, irrespective of the community or religion they come from, is familiar with this word. As Anupam was running a niche business, he thought that a brand name synonymous with the category would give more mileage.

Anupam decided to change the name of his website from Sagai.com to Shaadi.com. Unfortunately, the domain name Shaadi.com was already taken by someone. However, luckily, the person agreed to sell it to Anupam for $25,000. Anupam, who had saved $30,000 for running his business, paid $25,000 to buy the domain name. At that time, everyone thought Anupam was crazy.

According to Seth Godin, 'Marketing is a contest for people's attention.' In a busy marketplace, the name Shaadi.com stands out and has an excellent recall value. If Anupam had chosen some other name, he would have had to spend much more money to gain people's attention and make that brand name popular. Over time, Anupam has been lauded multiple times for this decision.

BUSINESS LESSONS

One can learn several important business lessons from the evolution of the brand Shaadi.com. A few of them are as follows.

Prioritise your market segment carefully

In every market there are different segments. Customers in every market segment have different behaviours and requirements. Reaching out to the segment that is ready to listen to you is more effective than interrupting the segment that is not.

During the early 2000s, internet penetration in India was very low. Moreover, matrimony being a culturally loaded subject, it was difficult to convince people in India to upload their profiles on a website. On the other hand, in the USA, during the dot-com bubble, internet usage and adoption accelerated quickly. Moreover, there was a bigger need for a service like Shaadi.com amongst the NRIs in countries like the USA and the UK, simply because these people were geographically distant from India, yet were looking to get married within their respective communities. But the absence of an organised source of information made it challenging for them.

Anupam targeted the US market as his first segment. Non-resident Indians were a small percentage of the overall US population, and there were very few Indian brands that had cross-border relevance. Therefore, the advertising inventory of Indian TV channels targeting the NRI audience was in low demand and within budget. To create brand awareness, the company aggressively ran advertisements on Indian TV channels in the US. It also targeted many local events, conferences and fairs. After a few years, when the US market was established, Anupam focused on the UK market.

After gaining popularity and building a substantial user base in the US and UK markets, Shaadi.com started marketing campaigns in India. With the advent of global companies like Yahoo followed by Google and Facebook, Indian consumers started becoming internet friendly. Around the year 2004, Anupam himself appeared in the first Indian TV commercial with an objective of building trust in the brand. To target the offline segment, the company started opening retail outlets called Shaadi Centres in 2004. These centres across various Indian cities acted as the offline face of an online company, which helped get on board parents who were hesitant about using the internet to find a match for their children.

Later, the emergence of many Indian online ventures like MakeMyTrip and Flipkart contributed to the growth of an internet-friendly audience. After 2010, smartphones further accelerated internet penetration and along with this, the growth of Shaadi.com's customer base also accelerated.

Use marketing partnerships to gain exposure

Good partnerships require people to identify and understand each other's needs, and create solutions that deliver satisfaction to customers and benefit both parties involved. It's a great way to increase brand awareness and customer acquisition in an inexpensive way.

In its early days, Shaadi.com didn't have much money for marketing, so it explored both conventional and unconventional partnerships that could increase its brand awareness. In the early 2000s, Yahoo was one of the biggest internet brands and was almost like a gateway to the internet. Shaadi.com saw the opportunity and partnered with Yahoo. This partnership enabled users of the Yahoo India portal to access various products and services on Shaadi.com, like wedding planners, mahurats, astrology, gifting and honeymoon travel. Through this partnership, Yahoo got something new to engage its Indian audience and Shaadi.com gained visibility among Indians who were users of Yahoo.

In the late 2000s, Shaadi.com explored a few interesting partnerships to reach out to new customer bases, including offline users. When smartphones and apps were not yet in vogue, Shaadi.com partnered with Vodafone and launched 'Shaadi.com on Vodafone'. A first-of-its-kind service in India, this tie-up enabled Vodafone customers to access Shaadi.com's matrimonial services on their mobile phones through a call, SMS or on Vodafone live! This concept became popular as 'Matrimony on the Move', as Vodafone users were able to search and view profiles of other members without needing to log on to the internet through a computer.

During the same period, Shaadi.com partnered with DishTV and launched a new interactive service on its platform called 'Shaadi Active'. This service made it possible for DishTV subscribers to look for profiles of prospective life partners listed on Shaadi.com on their TV screens. A subscriber could search for profiles based on criteria such as age, community, caste, profession, etc. The Shaadi.com profiles were displayed on the TV screen, and the subscriber could contact the person they liked. To ensure novelty, the profiles were refreshed daily.

Shaadi.com also partnered with television channel Star Plus for its matrimonial reality show Star Vivaah. Through this partnership, Shaadi.com offered participants an opportunity to choose from a well-researched collection of profiles that could be the closest match for their specific requirements. A lot of swayamvars were organised in various cities, which helped Shaadi.com build a relationship with its target audience.

There have been many other such partnerships that have helped the company reach its target audience and create brand awareness. Gourav Rakshit, the CEO of Shaadi.com, mentioned that one of the biggest strengths of his team is agility. Since its early days, the company has attracted many progressive brands for partnerships, as the team has been quick to come up with innovative and engaging content as per the requirement of partner brands.

Educate your customers

Regis McKenna once said, 'The best marketing is education.' While creating new markets, one of the basic requirements is to educate customers and define new industry standards.

In India, people have been using traditional matchmaking channels for ages and have been a little conservative about the topic. Getting people to register on Shaadi.com by simply telling them to come online and find a match was very difficult. While facing the challenges in market creation, Anupam also realised that the media found his concept newsworthy and wanted to discover more about it. He became very open to having conversations with the media and met many journalists one on one.

The media is one of the most trustworthy channels to educate customers. Based on authenticity, it shares your story and helps in establishing your credibility. During the initial days of Shaadi.com, Anupam spent almost 20 per cent of his time talking to the media. He was active in discussions around the topic on radio channels, TV shows and hosted many programmes. Over time, several prestigious channels like the BBC covered Anupam, the online matchmaking concept and Shaadi.com.

Anupam says, 'Creating awareness through media was more of an evolution, it was not something that happened much by design.' He was focused, persistent and determined in terms of sharing his thoughts and with time, opportunities presented themselves.

Apart from educating people about the concept of online matchmaking, Anupam has played an instrumental role in building the digital ecosystem in India. He is one of the founding members and past chairman of the Internet and Mobile Association of India (IAMAI). He is also one of the first investors in dozens of internet-based startups, including the Indian unicorn Ola Cabs.

Because of his initiatives to support disruption and innovation, Anupam has become a known personal brand. According to him, a personal brand is like a double-edged sword. It helps in 'starting things' as it attracts many people towards you for partnerships, investments, employment, etc. However, it also creates problems in 'running things' as it comes in the way when you roll up your sleeves and work along with your team. In a working environment, sometimes people look at you differently or get intimidated and don't open up. Anupam says, 'It's very important to learn to manage your personal brand.'

To educate its target audience, Shaadi.com also runs a portal called ShaadiLive. It's a blog that shares recent updates about the company, success stories, matchmaking trends, tips, product enhancements, etc.

Create initiatives with a higher purpose

Initiatives with higher purposes not only create awareness around a cause but also bring attention to your brand. Most importantly, they pull people towards a company rather than the company pushing its messages to capture the target audience.

In a country like India, marriage is not just a relationship between two people, it is a relationship between two families. For a brand like Shaadi.com, it is important to connect not only with people looking to get married but with everyone in the family. Gourav says, 'As a brand, Shaadi.com is primarily focused on celebrating everything around love, life and marriage first and then matchmaking.' Over the last few years, Shaadi.com has launched many campaigns, to represent the consciousness of Indian consumers and facilitate conversations among its audience on the topics they think and believe in. 'Tapping into something that people really value and think about has helped in establishing brand connect with a wider set of audience,' says Gourav. This becomes clearer if we look at some of the campaigns run by the brand.

To help raise awareness about dowry harassment in India, in 2012, Shaadi.com launched Angry Brides, an online flash-based browser game on Facebook. The landing page of the game shows an eight-armed woman, clad in red and resembling the powerful female Hindu goddess Durga, with various common household items like frying pans, rolling pins, broomsticks and stiletto heels in her hands. In this game, players strike grooms who demand a large dowry. Each hit lowers the amount demanded and if the player manages to bring the dowry to zero, they can proceed to the next level. This game received a great response on social media and was awarded by IAMAI for the best use of internet for social and economic development.

On Karwa Chauth, wives in India keep a day-long fast for the long life of their husbands. In 2014, the company launched a Karwa Chauth campaign – 'Fast for Her'. This initiative set out to take a stand and promote equality in marriage and urged men to express their love, gratitude and respect towards their wives by pledging to fast for their long life.

In 2015, the company launched a 'Dowry Calculator', which people could use to calculate the amount of dowry they deserve based on their educational qualifications, salary, etc. When the company first promoted this initiative, it received a strong backlash on social media for openly promoting the practice of dowry. However, soon enough people found out the truth behind this initiative. When someone entered his details in the calculator, what showed up wasn't the amount of dowry the person supposedly deserved but the dowry deaths statistics for India. This calculator attracted viewers from over 170 countries and created a lot of conversation among people on various online platforms.

In 2016, the company organised a digital campaign, 'Not for Sale', around the topic of dowry. Usually, the topic of dowry brings images of crying girls and pleading families to one's mind. But there is another side—the perspective of the boy. Even though the groom is at the centre of this 'transaction', no one focuses on him. This campaign gave boys a platform to express themselves without any pressure from their elders. The team used images and videos to mobilise support from young Indian singles on social media as well as the company's matchmaking platform.

In our society, physical attributes are given a lot of importance. To encourage its members to look beyond these factors and make a better decision for themselves, in 2017, Shaadi.com removed fields such as 'Complexion' and 'Body Type' from partner preferences. The company launched a campaign, 'Wanted Fair Brides and Grooms', to let people know that love comes in all shapes and shades. To sensitise people towards this, the company also launched a video in which a young poet Aranya Johar in her poem *A Brown Girl's Guide to Beauty* spoke about a girl's struggle with societal norms and conventions about body shape and complexion.

By thinking on behalf of the people and creating campaigns to uplift society, the company has been able to gain a lot of love and following for the brand, which is reflected in the audience engagement on the company's social media platforms. Though marriage is considered a private topic in India, by establishing brand connect with a wider audience, Shaadi.com has become one of the top Indian brands in terms of popularity and engagement, on social media platforms like Facebook.

Fail fast but strive for success

When technology is new, the market is new, the number of consumers is less and there is a reluctance in adopting a new approach, failures are more common than successes.

Shaadi.com is one of the earliest internet-based ventures in India. It started when Indian consumers were not used to online businesses and there were no proven case studies to fall back on for guidance. Also, the company's business model required changing customer behaviour around the culturally loaded topic of matrimony. 'We made tons of mistakes, but we learnt from every mistake. The faster we failed, the better we got,' says Gourav.

To bounce back from every failure with a new learning, Shaadi.com has focused on developing a culture of adaptation and agility within the organisation. Moreover, old rules of success don't give the same results, therefore, one must continuously unlearn old rules and relearn new ones to stay relevant in the continuously changing environment.

If we look holistically, technology is evolving, so is society and customer behaviour. People's outlook towards choosing their life partner is changing too. To keep up and stay ahead with evolutions in various areas, Shaadi.com is also continuously evolving. In the beginning, the platform was more like the classified section of a newspaper with very limited features. With time, the company kept on adding new features that allowed for greater interactivity and more robust privacy and security. When the company realised that users were becoming inclined towards chat messengers, it developed its own messaging system that let users interact in real time. Over two decades, the company has built a vast database of the marriageable population based on multiple parameters such as religion, community, profession, financial status, education, age, etc. The company keeps on analysing this data to come up with new insights around consumer behaviour.

With time, consumers started moving from desktops to smartphones. The desktop-to-mobile transition was not only the transition of technology, but also of consumer expectations. For instance, when people would access the internet on their desktops, they would take out dedicated time to browse websites. Almost like having a full meal in one go. But nowadays, people consume the internet through mobile phones in smaller chunks, like consuming small snacks regularly. This rapid change in consumer behaviour has compelled companies to be obsessed with relevance to the consumer. If a consumer is not hooked on in a few seconds, they can go to an alternative option with just a click. Keeping this in perspective, the company developed its mobile app that offered many additional features and functionalities compared to its website. Today, approximately 30 per cent of traffic on Shaadi.com comes via its app.

To sustain its culture, the company is focused on retaining its employees, who act as ambassadors of its culture when new employees join the company. Over time, various functions within the company have developed their own manuals that help new employees learn from the past experiences of older employees and help older employees in avoiding past mistakes in the future. Also, the things that worked in the past or in one market may not necessarily work in the future or in all markets as consumers may have different expectations. To stay relevant in the ever-changing environment, the team continuously revises and enhances these manuals based on new learnings.

Earn the trust of your customers

People prefer a brand or recommend it to others because of their trust in that brand. Though there is always scope for improvement, customers appreciate and trust a brand when they see it genuinely trying to make things better for them.

The Shaadi.com team worked hard to create trust around the brand through continuous value additions to their product. Anupam says, 'As a culture, everyone within the organisation is focused on giving his or her best to help our users. The team's efforts are reflected in continuous improvements in every area of business.'

The company has been continuously working towards providing better product experience for its users. One of the aspects of product experience is the availability of relevant profiles for every user. People may have specific requirements when it comes to their preferred life partner. For instance, a user may prefer someone from, say, South Mumbai while another may want someone from a particular profession, like a dentist. And while things are slowly changing in our society, caste may be a criterion for some people. As and when the analytics team finds weakness in the critical mass number of any criteria, it runs targeted campaigns to create the database. Presence of sufficient profiles in every community attracts more users and creates a virtuous cycle.

As marriage is a socially and culturally sensitive topic, people have been concerned about sharing their personal information on the internet. To address the concerns around information security, the company has taken certification from TRUSTe, a privacy seal for safety and confidentiality of user data, and

VeriSign, secure site seal for security of payments and credit card information. To ensure that quality systems and processes are in place, the company has obtained an ISO 9001:2000 certification.

To bring down marriage-related frauds, every profile is screened for authenticity by the CRM team before making it available on the portal. All uploaded photographs are screened to ensure that they are genuine and don't violate socially acceptable norms, and controls have been provided to users to make their photos visible based on certain filters and password protection. To maintain privacy, members control the visibility of their contact details, and only verified numbers are made available. In addition, a combination of supervised and unsupervised algorithms runs in the back end for reviewing profiles, manual screening and digital verification.

Furthermore, to report any misuse or misconduct by a member, the portal has an abuse control button that alerts the Shaadi.com team to any issues that may need to be investigated. To reduce any misuse, the team is also working on integration of social media profiles with its platform. The company has also created a strong and credible deterrent by working with the Cyber Crime units and local law enforcement agencies.

The Match Guarantee feature provided on the platform guarantees money back, if a premium member doesn't receive even a single acceptance within 30 days of expressing interest in at least ten members. Also, the e-matchmaker tool on the portal matches profiles among the millions of listed profiles based on various algorithms. To cater to a specific segment of society that is less comfortable in directly reaching out to a prospective match, personalised membership plans—Select Shaadi and VIP Shaadi—have been launched. The USP of these programmes is intermediated matchmaking through a dedicated relationship advisor and complete discretion.

Once members are married, they don't need to revisit the portal, so their customer lifetime value is low. But through their word of mouth, they keep on sending new members and indirectly keep on contributing to their customer lifetime value. 'In our business, though the usage of product is short term, memory of usage is long term,' says Gourav. Every successful marriage through the portal is a marketing campaign as couples become brand ambassadors and talk about the role Shaadi.com played in getting them connected. As of December 2017, the company has over 5 million success stories. The positive reinforcement of results with success stories drives people to embrace Shaadi.com. Over 15,000 new members register each day, and the number is growing at approximately 20 per cent a year, broadly in line with the growth in internet penetration in the country.

Jack Dorsey said, 'The strongest thing you can cultivate as an entrepreneur is to not rely on luck but cultivating an ability to recognise fortunate situations when they are occurring.' The journey of Shaadi.com is a testament to this statement. As an entrepreneur, Anupam recognised a fortunate business opportunity in his personal problem and developed a simplified solution for millions of people looking to get married. Today, Shaadi.com is considered an iconic and innovative brand from India, but instead of resting on its success and laurels, the Shaadi.com team is keen to create better experiences for its customers. With time, the marketplace will continue to change, technology will continue to shift and the brand Shaadi.com will continue to evolve.

ANUPAM MITTAL

Advice from Anupam Mittal

- A good sales strategy means people want to buy from you and you choose to sell to them. To support this, the focus of marketing should be demand creation through pull, not push.
- There are two aspects of demand creation. The first aspect is building a great product or a great service. Good product or service leads to a lot of word of mouth and brings economics in your favour. The second aspect is building a great brand through great communication, consistent storytelling and consistent delivery of brand promise to customers.
- A lot of times, people mistake brand for advertising campaigns. Advertising is a form of communication that creates brand awareness; advertising does not mean brand. Customers have certain expectations from your business. The way you live up to those expectations defines your brand.
- By looking at big brands, entrepreneurs get tempted to get into multiple things quickly. This temptation is both dangerous and costly. Rather than broadening your base quickly, try to become the best in your niche first. You should be able to respect yourself more than anyone else in your niche.

Bringing back happy childhood memories

Let's face the reality. In today's overcrowded and highly competitive marketplace, dozens of new Fast Moving Consumer Goods (FMCG) are launched every day. With retailers' shelves already overflowing with existing products, brands find it difficult to differentiate their products. Moreover, the attention span of customers is reducing.

Within the FMCG industry, if we look at the beverage category, bigger players such as Coca-Cola, Pepsi and Dabur have been present in the market for years with their huge customer base, distribution network and resources that are difficult to match.

In such a tough market, a startup, Hector Beverages has rewritten the rules of the game and built a strong packaged beverage brand—Paper Boat. Launched in August 2013, Paper Boat has gone on to become one of the fastest growing FMCG brands in India. It managed to touch the pulse of Indian customers by providing Indian ethnic drinks using authentic recipes and refreshing packaging. Starting with two flavours, Jaljeera and Aam Panna, Paper Boat now has over a dozen varieties such as Jamun Kala Khatta, Aamras, Golgappe Ka Pani, Anar, Chilli Guava, etc. The brand has also introduced seasonal products such as Thandai, Serbet-e-khaas, Rose Tamarind and Panakam, among others.

In 2016, afaqs! ranked Paper Boat among the top 10 buzziest brands of India and in 2017, Interbrand recognised it as a breakthrough brand.

Today, Paper Boat drinks are sold across 1,20,000 outlets in markets like Delhi, Bengaluru, Pune, Hyderabad, Chennai, Mumbai and Kolkata. The company is now focusing on the brand's penetration in tier-2 towns across the country.

This chapter encapsulates the journey of Paper Boat, a brand with the mission to preserve and promote traditional Indian drinks that hold a special place in our childhood memories.

HOW THE JOURNEY BEGAN

The journey of the brand Paper Boat started with the search for Aam Panna, a traditional Indian summer drink. The company's co-founders, Neeraj Kakkar, James Nutall, Suhas Misra and Neeraj Biyani, would enjoy the homemade Aam Panna brought by Suhas, with lunch. They wanted to have more of it and wanted to share it with others. They searched for it in the market but couldn't find the drink anywhere. During this search, they found that many traditional homemade drinks, which they enjoyed in their childhood, were not available in the market. They realised that traditional drinks were slowly vanishing from people's lives and their recipes had to be preserved for the next generation.

With an objective to preserve traditional drinks and make them available in a hygienic and packaged form, they planned to launch their own ethnic beverage brand. The team test-marketed the product in February 2013 before launching the brand Paper Boat nationally in August 2013 with two flavours—Jaljeera and Aam Panna.

THE BRAND NAME: PAPER BOAT

Naming your product or service is the most important decision. If the name is memorable and can create a positive perception in the minds of customers, then it acts as a big differentiating factor in the crowded market.

All children make paper boats. Making them in the monsoons is a happy childhood memory. Creating your own paper boat gave you a sense of accomplishment, as a child. You felt sad when your paper boat got lost or drowned, and you also felt excited when you saw it staying afloat under harsh circumstances. The team wanted to evoke childhood memories through packaged Indian ethnic drinks so they decided to come up with a brand name that could instantly connect people with their childhood memories. The brand name Paper Boat appeared to be a perfect fit.

BUSINESS LESSONS

There are many important business lessons that can be learnt from the evolution of this brand.

Create a new category

Most often, companies introduce new brands in established categories and try to promote these brands via advertising. Even after spending a lot of money on advertising, these new brands are not able to develop a recall value as their categories are already crowded with established brands. One of the best ways to create a powerful brand is to create a new category where you can be the first.

Before the launch of Paper Boat, the Indian soft drink market was filled with categories such as carbonated drinks, sports drinks, energy drinks, juices and juice-based drinks. There was no category for Indian ethnic drink and no options other than cola, fizzy and preservatives-based drinks even if the customer was looking for it. Hector Beverages picked this opportunity and filled the gap by launching Paper Boat.

While creating a new category may sound simple, it is not. To establish a new category in the market, a lot of effort goes into educating people about the new category, creating new standards, setting up supply chains and distribution channels, applying innovation and creativity in product development and so on. But the benefit of creating a new category is that by being the first, a brand has a lot of scope to grow fast and establish itself as a market leader.

Develop a great product

One of the biggest competitive advantages of any company is the authenticity of its products. A great product is the foundation of a great brand and good-quality ingredients are the foundation of a great product.

The company has positioned Paper Boat as a premium brand. All Paper Boat drinks are made without preservatives, added colours or carbonation. These drinks are prepared using local spices, fruits, flowers and pulses. The quality of these ingredients plays a very important role in the quality of the end-products and Hector Beverages has been very selective in partnering with suppliers who can provide the best-quality ingredients.

To get the best ingredients, the company has been focusing on creating a robust supply chain. All the mangoes used in Paper Boat mango drinks are naturally processed, unlike the regular way of ripening mangoes in ethylene chambers. Right now, pomegranates for the anar drink come from California, the lemons are sourced from Europe and jamuns comes from Bihar and Maharashtra. The company has also tied up with an NGO that works on sourcing ingredients from the tribal regions of Madhya Pradesh. It has also been getting seeds of purple carrots from Turkey and sowing them in Ooty.

The company has two manufacturing plants, one at Manesar near Gurgaon and the other at Mysore. Both these plants are equipped to meet pharma-level standards of quality and hygiene.

To continuously innovate and improve its products, the company has looked beyond the standards of the FMCG industry and has picked up ideas and principles from diverse fields such as technology and fast fashion companies.

Like technology companies, it values customer feedback and tries to adapt, change and improve its products all the time. Hector Beverages has its R&D centre based in Bengaluru, where research on 15 products takes place simultaneously. It takes around two years for a product to hit the market. Based on the product's supply, shelf life, machinery requirement and market interest, the company launches, rejects or improves the products.

Hector Beverages has also been inspired by the way fast fashion retailer Zara introduces small special collections that remain on the rack for a short time. Hector Beverages comes up with special editions of Paper Boat drinks around festival time for about two weeks. For example, it launched Thandai during Holi, Panakam around Ram Navami, Kacchi Lassi around Baisakhi and Rose Sherbet during Ramzan. These occasional drinks have received great responses. The company is working on a plan to build a 12-month calendar to launch occasional drinks in every part of the country, every month.

The importance of effective product packaging

Packaging plays many important roles, like giving an image to a product, attracting customers, protecting products from contamination and spoilage, providing information about the product and price, facilitating transportation of product and so on. The packaging is the first point of contact with customers when they decide to purchase a product.

Paper Boat was awarded The India Story Design Award for Packaging Design. Its packaging is interesting, innovative and informative. It enables the serving of a traditional drink in a modern way and stands out in a cluttered market. For differentiation and authenticity, doypacks that look and feel like paper have been chosen. These packs provide the unique experience of gripping and holding the product while drinking. They are light, compact and easily transportable.

Even the cap of the package is an innovation. It is pilfer-proof, visually aligned with the package and completes its shape. It is user-friendly, that is, it can be opened with two fingers and is convenient to hold, turn and replace.

The packaging graphics reflect the simplicity and purity of the drink inside. Flat colours, curvilinear shape, and brief stories covering happy childhood memories contribute to delightful nostalgia and establish an emotional relationship with customers.

Additionally, these packs are approximately 50 per cent more cost-efficient than Tetra Pak. The pouches are made of a four-part laminate that makes the pack withstand extreme pressure and heat. The pouches have a 10 per cent lower carbon footprint and lower environmental impact than glass bottles, Tetra Pak cartons and PET bottles.

Over time, to meet the consumption patterns of different customers, the brand's packaging has evolved from 250 ml single serve doypacks to 500 ml and 1 litre multi-serve Tetra Pak cartons.

Differentiate your distribution strategy

Distribution is one of the key aspects of marketing strategy. Usually, new beverage brands try to convince departmental stores and kirana stores to stock their products. But kirana stores have only one cooler and departmental stores are already filled with many established brands.

Initially, instead of following the regular route, Hector Beverages approached Indigo airlines for a distribution partnership. The Indigo airlines team liked the product and felt that they could offer something new and different to their customers. Through this partnership, Paper Boat was able to get the attention of travellers during their private and captive time. People interacted with the beautiful and unique packaging, read stories on the pack and enjoyed Indian ethnic drinks. Also, many influencers discovered the brand during their travel with Indigo and talked about it on social media.

Later, the company partnered with modern retail stores such as Big Bazaar and Reliance Fresh, followed by partnerships with coffee chains like Barista Lavazza, hotels like Westin and Trident, and companies like Google, Facebook, LinkedIn and others.

To increase its reach in tier-2 towns, Hector Beverages tied up with Indo Nissin Foods (maker of Top Ramen noodles) that has a robust distribution network pan-India. As of now, Paper Boat is present in over 1,20,000 outlets in cities such as Delhi, Mumbai, Bangalore, Hyderabad, Pune and Chennai. Due to its increasing popularity, the brand is now available in more airlines, trains, modern retail stores and mom-and-pop stores. It has also partnered with e-commerce stores such as Amazon to sell a few of its products such as thandai, especially in multi-pack formats.

Focus on building relationships

Usually, companies spend a lot of money to create brand awareness by giving heavy discounts, engaging expensive endorsers and running print, outdoor and TV campaigns. The objective of these marketing campaigns is not only to create brand awareness, but also to establish an emotional connect and build relationships with customers.

Since its inception, Paper Boat's marketing campaigns have focused on building relationships with the target audience through storytelling and have followed a distinctive tone of creating nostalgia around childhood memories.

Initially, the team focused on selective channels and influential people rather than the target market as a whole. When a few influencers tried the brand during their flights with Indigo and talked about it on social media, the team tapped into conversations around these posts. Additionally, for over two years, the team wrote interesting letters and mails, which included poetry and childhood memories, to influencers and requested them to share their genuine feedback about the product. Many of them liked the product and posted about it on their social media accounts and blogs.

The team has been very active on various social media channels. Every day, they put up stories in the form of creative and fun-loving illustrations on Facebook, Twitter and Instagram, and keep on screening films, uploaded on YouTube.

These films don't talk about the brand, rather their storylines connect the audience with their childhood memories and dreams. These short films include *Rizwan, Hope – The Boat, When I Grow Up, Life Is Still Beautiful, My First Train Ride* and others around important days like Children's Day and Teachers' Day. At the start of 2017, the company collaborated with a few other startup founders and Sunidhi Chauhan to come up with a music video titled *Hum Honge Kaamyab*. It also released a short film *A Paper Boat Ride Down the River of Memories* with the glorious soundtrack from *Malgudi Days* and the voice of Gulzar, on both YouTube and television.

India is a country of festivals, and every festival has its own memories. Usually, brands give a special look to their products during festivals by changing their packaging. But Paper Boat decided to do something disruptive, it changed the product itself. The company deep dived into the entire year's festivals and converted festival periods into a marketing campaign— 'Appointment Launches'. As part of this campaign, the company launched relevant drinks, such as Thandai in North India around Holi, Panakam in South India around Rama Navami and so on. These drinks enjoyed high emotional value with customers and brought them closer to the brand.

Meeting customers, talking to them and building relationships help in planning the evolution of products. In early 2017, the company launched the 'Happy Patrol' campaign, a customer connect and sampling programme. The company recruited the smartest and sharpest young women from graduate colleges across seven cities as its brand ambassadors. These youngsters embodied the company's values such as honesty, positivity, intelligence and readiness to put a smile on everyone's face. Every weekend, they connected with their target audience at modern retail stores to share a sample of the product and have conversations around the brand. This two-way dialogue helped them hear from the target audience and understand their perspectives better. Starting with Bengaluru, the campaign has slowly made its way to Mumbai, Pune, Hyderabad, Chennai and a few areas of Punjab and Jammu. In a year's time, the team of 300 brand ambassadors had met around 50,000 customers directly and the brand was able to strengthen its relationship with its customers.

Many of us have cherished postcards from our childhood, and the memory of postmen delivering them is etched with nostalgia. In 2014, the brand launched the 'Postcard Campaign', to bring the younger generation closer to their parents. The company placed replicas of postboxes in select office canteens, all over the country. Right next to these boxes, the company put up designed postcards, which were made by Paper Boat in association with the Indian Postal Service. All people had to do was write letters to their parents, on these postcards, and put them in the 'postbox'. Paper Boat would take care of the postage and delivery. To promote this campaign, the company launched a film on YouTube narrating the story of a boy and his father. It covers the boy's childhood days as well as his adult life, where he is living in a city far from home.

Value customer feedback

It is important to collect and analyse customer feedback. This feedback helps an organisation know what is liked by consumers and what needs to be improved. Fixing any highlighted issues helps in maintaining relationships, and sometimes feedback provides valuable ideas beneficial for business.

There is no single ethnic drink, and every drink has a different formula waiting to be discovered. Through trial and error, the Paper Boat team has been creating drinks that have been lost to the past. It has kept an open mind and sought a variety of opinions. After the flavour is in place, the team is willing to adjust the formula to meet customers' expectations. The company launches drinks in selective regions and then scales up their production and distribution based on feedback. As and when required, the company works on improvising the drinks to meet its customers' expectations.

The team actively observes social media. It not only collects people's memories but also acts on their concerns. For example, when a few people mentioned on twitter that it was difficult to open the cap of the doypack, the team reworked the cap and came up with a better option.

Earn your credentials

Evidences and references based on genuine substance can help a startup earn credibility in the market. People infer that a startup is credible if it has ingredients such as experienced leaders, backing from known investors, coverage by popular media channels, acceptance by reputable distributors, word of mouth by influencers and so on.

The leadership team of Hector Beverages has impressive credentials and relevant experience in various areas of business. Right at the beginning, in 2011, the company raised funds from Infosys founder N.R. Narayana Murthy's venture capital fund Catamaran. A few other leading venture capital firms, such as Footprint Ventures, Sequoia Capital, Sofina and Hillhouse Capital, have invested in the company.

Luminaries like Vir Sanghvi and Harish Bhatt have mentioned positive things about the brand in their posts. The company's CEO Neeraj Kakkar has been a fellow at INK, India's foremost platform for the exchange of cutting-edge ideas and inspiring stories. His talk during the annual INK conference has been viewed more than 35,000 times. He has also been a speaker at many popular and prestigious conferences.

Articles in media are perceived more believable than advertisements. Paper Boat has received a lot of favourable coverage by reputed media platforms such as Forbes and Mint, and it has also been covered extensively by various bloggers.

So far, the team's experimental mindset has paid huge dividends and has created a lovable brand of Indian ethnic drinks. In terms of international expansion, the brand has started increasing its presence in markets like the Middle East, Singapore, UK and USA. Along with the expansion of portfolio of Indian ethnic drinks, Neeraj's vision has been to create a similar model for Mexican, Korean and other regional drinks across the world. In terms of brand extension, the company has launched chikki as a new product, and is in the process of launching Paper Boat branded aam pappad.

To manage its next phase of growth, the company is focusing on making both its supply chain and its distribution channels robust. It would be interesting to see how this brand evolves in its next phase of growth.

Advice from Neeraj Kakkar

- Be authentic. Don't overpromise. Be transparent and keep things human.
- Look at marketing not as a one-way dialogue but as a way to engage customers in meaningful conversations.

NEERAJ KAKKAR
paper boat

Satisfying the needs of foodies

Steve Jobs often said, 'We're here to put a dent in the universe.' If you look closely, you will find a few interesting brands that have made a mark in their sphere of influence. One of these brands is the food-tech titan Zomato, that has put a dent in the universe of foodies.

Started as an idea in a company's cafeteria in 2008, within a decade, Zomato became one of the world's largest restaurant search and food delivery platforms. It has a presence in 24 countries, and it is a market leader in 18 of them. More than 1.4 million restaurants in over 10,000 cities are listed on Zomato, and every month more than 120 million people seeking to satisfy their food related needs visit the platform.

Zomato has won The Economic Times Startup of the Year Award and has been consistently ranked as one of India's fastest growing technology companies in the Deloitte Technology

Fast 50 report. It has been backed by many leading investors, including the Indian internet giant Info Edge, the Indian arm of Sequoia Capital, Silicon Valley based Vy Capital, Singapore based Temasek Holdings and the Chinese internet giant Alibaba.

THE BEGINNING OF THE JOURNEY

The journey started around 2008, when Deepinder Goyal was working as a consultant at the Delhi office of Bain & Company. This was a time when he and his colleagues had to queue up to look at a stack of menu cards at the company's cafeteria, just so they could decide what food to order from the nearby restaurants. There was only one copy of each menu and they couldn't take these menu cards to their desks because if they lost them, then nobody would be able to order food. Just to see the menu and order the food, they had to spend a long time waiting for others to finish placing their orders.

To ensure that everyone was able to view the menu cards on their computers, Deepinder scanned the cards and uploaded them onto the company's intranet portal. His colleagues reacted positively to this little initiative. By looking at the frequency of visits and the utility of the service, he decided to scale up this service and spread it beyond the office cafeteria and convinced his office colleague and friend Pankaj Chaddah to join him. Over the weekends, they started gathering menus of restaurants in the Delhi NCR region and started Foodiebay.com, an online collection of restaurant menus.

By the latter half of 2009, the website gained some traction and user feedback was excellent. Soon restaurants began contacting the Foodiebay team to advertise on the site, and that's how the revenue stream began. When it started getting difficult for Deepinder and Pankaj to manage both office work and the venture, they decided to quit their jobs and work full-time on their startup. In late 2010, the name of Foodiebay was changed to Zomato.

THE BRAND NAME: ZOMATO

While being bootstrapped for around two years, Foodiebay had passed many milestones, such as serving close to 2 million customers, expanding its presence to new cities like Pune and Bengaluru, and building a listing of more than 8,000 restaurants on their website. In 2010, Sanjeev Bikhchandani, the founder of Info Edge, India's largest internet classifieds company that runs portals like Naukri.com, Jeevansathi.com and 99acres.com, came across Foodiebay as a user. He liked the concept and sent an email to Deepinder to arrange a meeting. Deepinder jumped at the opportunity and within 3 hours of receiving the mail, he met Sanjeev and within 48 hours, received the first round of funding of $1 million from Info Edge.

After getting financial backing from Info Edge, the team's vision started becoming bigger. They wanted to expand the business to new markets, evolve the product from just restaurant listings to a recommendation engine and start new sections like nightlife. Deepinder and Pankaj felt that the brand name Foodiebay would restrict their positioning to food, and venturing into any adjacencies such as nightlife would be difficult. Also, Ambarish Raghuvanshi, the CFO of Info Edge then, made Deepinder and his team realise that the last four letters of Foodiebay contained the name of another prominent internet company—eBay—so potential trademark issues could appear in the future. Considering these two strategic reasons, the team decided to give away their established brand name.

For the new brand name, the team wanted to keep the idea of food in focus and pick a name that was short, easy to remember and not limited by the time of day. Eventually, the team zeroed in on the name Zomato, which had a zing to it and was originally a play on the word tomato. This name sounded lively, was not restricted to food, and had a great recall value.

Much to the team's surprise, the domain name Zomato. com was available for $10,000. Deepinder didn't want to spend this much money on purchasing a domain name. He was planning to save money and buy another domain name Forkwise.com, which was available for just $10. But Ambarish advised Deepinder not to leave the catchy name Zomato.com and offered to buy it for him personally. Seeing Ambarish's confidence in the name, Deepinder went ahead and purchased the domain name Zomato.com.

BUSINESS LESSONS

There are many important business lessons that can be learnt from the evolution of the Zomato brand. A few of them are as follows.

Scale up your vision as you scale up your business

Once, two men were laying bricks and a man walked up and asked both the men what they were doing. The first man answered, 'I am laying bricks' and the second one answered, 'I am building a cathedral.' Both men were doing the same work, but one had a narrow vision while the other had a broader view. Vision is all about looking at your product and business beyond the day-to-day operations with a larger purpose in mind. Once the initial vision of the business begins to gain success, its leaders gain the confidence to scale up their vision, which leads to a cycle of growth.

After the success of his idea within his office, Deepinder scaled up his vision and decided to cover the whole of Delhi NCR and by July 2008, over 1,200 restaurants in the region were listed on the site. He scaled up his vision further and started expanding from one city to multiple cities in India. By 2010, restaurants in Pune and Bengaluru were added to the website, followed by Chennai, Hyderabad, Ahmedabad and Chandigarh. By 2012, Zomato had covered over 40,000 restaurants in 12 cities in India and had evolved itself just from a restaurant discovery website to a platform with features like restaurant reviews. It had on board over 1,000 advertising clients and had created a profitable business model.

Scaling up its vision further, Zomato decided to enter international markets. In September 2012, Zomato entered Dubai followed by various markets in Asia Pacific, Europe and America. As every market is different in terms of regulations, user behaviour and food culture, the company faced multiple challenges in expanding to new markets. To overcome these challenges, Zomato set up local offices in the respective countries and hired local staff led by entrepreneurial country managers, who understood Zomato's culture and were responsible for driving growth in their respective markets.

Success in easier-to-win markets gave the team the confidence to enter tougher markets. In many markets, Zomato expanded organically, but to speed up its growth in a few markets where similar products existed, it focused on inorganic growth and acquired the existing players. After becoming one of the global leaders in its niche and building a very profitable business model around ad sales, the team decided to enter other niches around food, such as food delivery and table reservations. To strengthen its position in the food delivery segment, Zomato acquired home chef aggregator TinMen and a food delivery startup Runnr. It also built alliances with many big and small players to provide a larger variety of healthy meal options to its users.

Scaling up its vision further, Zomato acquired the US-based restaurant reservations and table-management platform NexTable and launched Zomato Book, a table booking service which lets its users make, modify and cancel bookings online even when a restaurant is closed. This service gave restaurant managers real-time insights to maximise their seating capacity, estimate occupancy and offer notifications to wait-listed customers in case a table became available.

As Zomato was continuously scaling up its business, it also continuously scaled up its vision to achieve more. To sustain its vision for growth, the team from top to bottom works on the mindset of '1% done' and considers that it is just getting started. No matter how many milestones have been achieved, the team considers that it has achieved only 1 per cent and always remembers that its destination is a moving target.

Keep your ears to the ground

It is important for an entrepreneur and their team to pay attention to everything that is happening around them and to what people are saying. During its initial days, Deepinder and Pankaj met restaurant owners to understand their challenges, met top food bloggers to understand how they discovered restaurants and what they looked for in them, and they even talked to customers coming out of restaurants. The insights from these discussions in various cities helped them in setting up a strong business foundation and creating a world-class product. As the business started scaling up in multiple cities and countries, they created teams to take regular feedback from various stakeholders in the ecosystem.

Given that restaurant menus can change on a regular basis, old restaurants could close down and restaurant names or locations could change, the Zomato team visits every restaurant in the city and updates restaurant-related information such as name, menu, location, etc. every three months. Imagine the effort that goes into this activity, to update the information on 1.4 million restaurants in over 10,000 cities in 24 countries. Moreover, this number is continuously increasing.

The Zomato team almost never misses an opportunity to speak with restaurant owners and take valuable insights to evolve their product. For instance, once, new restaurant owners shared with the team that before they got an opportunity to fully stabilise their operations, their restaurants' ratings on Zomato would start to drop. They were looking for valuable customer feedback to improve themselves, but a few bad reviews due to initial operational challenges were becoming a death sentence. To help new restaurants navigate their early days better, new restaurants started getting a 'beta period' of 60 days. Now, the ratings of new restaurants start showing up after 60 days, and reviews gathered during this period do not count towards the overall rating. This way restaurants get valuable feedback from their customers, which helps them fix problems without worrying about a low rating.

Zomato strongly focuses on building its online community and is in constant touch with users to get feedback to improve the product. For example, by listening to its community of users, the team got to know about their concerns around Zomato's restaurant rating logic. Earlier, these ratings were determined by the weighted average of absolute scores, which resulted in the clustering of ratings within a range. But users wanted to compare two restaurants to decide which one was a better option. To solve this concern, Zomato moved from an absolute rating to a classroom-style grading model, where the distribution of scores in every city was normalised, resulting in ratings in each city being distributed over a normal curve.

Another interesting example is how the team, through a survey amongst its users, found that given a choice, the users would prefer to eat at or order from a restaurant that is clean and hygienic. To address this need gap, and to better educate its users, Zomato introduced Food Hygiene Ratings for the listed restaurants. Similarly, when a fire at restaurants in the Kamala Mills compound, Mumbai, led to 14 deaths, some pertinent questions about fire safety at restaurants were raised. Zomato announced an initiative to display the fire safety certificate of restaurants on its platform. Thus, the Zomato team continuously develops its understanding of the evolving market and user expectations, and keeps adding new features accordingly.

Choose your battles wisely

Every new market is a new battlefield with a new set of competitors and customer expectations. The things that work in one market may not work in others. Deepinder says, 'It is very important for you to pick up the right battles. If any battle is going to kill you, then it's better to change the battle and remain alive.'

After Zomato had captured all the high-growth cities in India, it wanted to enter the next phase of growth. It had two options—either to expand within the Indian market by entering other food-related verticals such as food delivery, or continue to grow as a restaurant search and review platform in international markets. In both cases, new learnings were required in the form of understanding new business models and markets. Restaurant search is not a capital-intensive business and has strong network effect for local advertisers and users, whereas food delivery is a high-burn business model.

As the dynamics of every business model are different, instead of diversifying into a new area, Zomato decided to focus on expanding its existing business in international markets. The company created a team of two members who would scout new markets for expansion opportunities. The team evaluated markets on various criteria such as market size, product market fit, internet penetration rate, spoken language, eating out habits, socio-economic factors like cost of labour, and advertising channels used by restaurants. The team also checked on existing competitors and their products. After proper research, the team picked up selective markets where there were more chances of winning with minimal changes in the product.

Considering that Dubai is one of the most accepted business as well as tourist destinations, with a lively restaurant industry and an extremely multicultural and tech-savvy population, Zomato chose it as the first global destination for expansion. The quick success in Dubai gave the team a false sense of confidence, and the company quickly expanded into many other markets such as Sharjah and Abu Dhabi in the UAE followed by Sri Lanka, Qatar, the Philippines, South Africa and the UK. Along with its rapid expansion, the company also faced a few setbacks that helped the team understand that the battle in every market was very different from the battles in the markets of India and Dubai. Zomato put in a lot of effort into localising and customising the product according to every new market and tasted success again.

In 2013, Zomato was launched in New Zealand, but the service didn't catch on as quickly as the company had hoped. This was because a local competitor—MenuMania —dominated the market. As the restaurant search business has strong network effects, moving the traffic from an established platform to its own platform was a difficult battle. Instead of putting in effort, time and burning cash in capturing market share from the competitor, Zomato decided to grow inorganically and acquired MenuMania. Zomato integrated the MenuMania product along with its interesting features and switched the traffic to the Zomato platform.

Seeing positive results from its first acquisition, the Zomato team started finding local monopolistic players in various markets. Deepinder says, 'We looked for companies that had a strong hold in their regions and were available at lower valuation.' In the same year, Zomato acquired four competitors in Europe: Cibando in Italy, Lunchtime in Czech Republic, Obedovat in Slovakia and Gatronauci in Poland followed by a few others in the upcoming years. As its largest acquisition, in 2015, Zomato acquired Urbanspoon, which was three times in size (in terms of traffic). Through this acquisition, Zomato became the Number 1 player in Australia and Number 2 player in the US and Canada markets. These acquisitions have added many new localised business models, more content and traffic, and interesting product features to Zomato, making it probably the largest restaurant search company in the world.

After winning many battles in the restaurant search business and establishing a sustainable revenue model, Zomato decided to enter other business models in and around food such as food delivery and table reservations. Interestingly, as users visit Zomato naturally to consume content around menus, reviews, ratings, photos, etc., the company had to spend minimally on customer acquisition and marketing for its new business models as compared to any of its competitors.

Evaluate your options with effort vs impact analysis

A marketer can choose from among numerous channels to reach out to its target segment. But every channel requires a different level of effort and moves the needle differently. Pramod Rao, Head of Growth at Zomato, says, 'A marketer should identify low-effort and high-impact opportunities. At the same time, [they] should not neglect high effort, high-impact opportunities for long-term results.'

Zomato is a viral product as it surrounds a necessity—food. To attract foodies in its early days, the team tried many low-cost ways to expand its user base. Understanding that the early adopters would come from corporates, the team members convinced their friends in various companies to change their messenger status to one that mentioned food and Zomato. They also pushed their friends to send emails to their colleagues and put Zomato stickers at restaurants they visited. To build a growing community of foodies and brand advocates, Zomato capitalised on social media and built a huge and loyal following on various social media channels largely due to its witty and design-intensive posts around food.

Facebook is used more as a platform for updates about things such as new TV commercials, official blog posts, photo albums from events conducted by Zomato and so on. Because Twitter allows for real-time conversation, it is used daily to respond to queries from people asking for recommendations. The company also periodically runs contests on Twitter, Foodie Friday being one of the most popular contests that has been running for many years now.

To create a large food community and add a social aspect to the recommendation engine, the company integrated social features into its website. Once a user logs into Zomato using their Facebook or Google account, the website automatically pulls out a list of the user's social media friends already registered on Zomato. Users can follow their friends and get notifications about their activities like reviews, ratings, favourites and recommendations.

To target a segment that would appreciate the paperback guide on good food around them, in 2012, in collaboration with Citibank, Zomato launched the 'Citibank Zomato Restaurant Guide'. This guide was very different from the existing options in the market and was positioned as a unique 'occasion' based guide that recommended restaurants based on different needs. This guide was a huge hit and helped in establishing Zomato's authority in the restaurant space. Later, when the impact of this effort started getting saturated, the company discontinued it.

To keep its users engaged, the company tried many low-effort and high-impact initiatives on its website. Based on user data, on a weekly basis, it came up with a list of top 25 trending restaurants in the city. To reward (virtually) people who are the most active and respected members of the Zomato community, the company started highlighting seasoned foodies with titles like Foodie, Big Foodie, Super Foodie and Connoisseur. The leaderboard on the site showcases the top reviewers in different locations and encourages friendly competition between users for entering the top 25 slots on the leaderboard.

With the advent of smartphones, people began to share photographs of food dishes served in restaurants on social networks and the term 'food porn' became popular. The team realised that the porn domain (.xxx) was an untapped opportunity and thought to combine the idea of food and porn and play on the social media term 'food porn'. Zomato started Zomato.xxx, the world's first .xxx domain site dedicated solely to delicious food. The purpose of the site is to share the most popular photos (of food) posted by users on Zomato's actual website or app. This has become a nice and humorous endeavour and today, many users look up these pictures before deciding where to eat.

To target the user base in various cities, the company ran many localised marketing activities such as marathons, including FoodSprint in Delhi and Zomathon in Bangalore. The company also organised Yummy Yatra in conjunction with The Pet Pujaris, a Mumbai-based group of food enthusiasts. It was a fun activity that engaged active foodies, also known as Pujaris, who head to new destinations and discover multiple eateries over the weekend. On similar lines, many other localised activities created a lot of ambassadors for the brand.

As a marketing channel, TV has the power to reach the masses but it is a known fact that television commercials can cost a bomb. Rather than creating a TV commercial through the traditional and expensive way of hiring an agency, in 2012, Zomato came up with a TVC 'The last wish' which was to be a crowd-sourcing contest with a prize money of ₹5 Lakh. This competition was open to everyone from amateur videographers to advertising agencies. This contest created a lot of visibility for the brand and a lot of followers and advocates on social media. Out of over 90 submissions, a young team from Chennai was selected as the winner. The 20-second video was aired at primetime on Star World and NDTV Good Times.

In 2015, when the company entered the food delivery segment and was looking to ramp-up its late-night orders, it decided to associate with another late-night activity—porn browsing. Based on an insight that India ranks fifth in the amount of daily visitors to the popular explicit content website PornHub, Zomato decided to target these users to get them to click on late night food delivery services and started advertising on pornography websites in India. The creative team designed some ads with double meanings to strike a chord with their target audience. The ads ran from 11 p.m. to 4 a.m. and reached the target audience at a much lower cost as compared to other online advertising platforms. Later, these advertisements were stopped as the team sensed that they had crossed the fine line between marketing irreverence and cultural insensitivity.

By 2015, Zomato had already become a strong brand in the restaurant search space through its low-cost marketing activities. As the user base had become large, similar efforts were not creating a high impact in terms of user growth rate. To increase the impact of its efforts and communicate at a mass scale, the company decided to spend some money on TV commercials. This time, the scale of business and objective was significantly different than that of the erstwhile crowdsourcing campaign, and the company wanted the best in the industry to work on it. They worked with the advertising agency Ogilvy & Mather and came up with two commercials directed by Shoojit Sircar, an Indian film director and producer who has directed movies like *Vicky Donor, Madras Cafe* and *Piku*. These campaigns received a very favourable response on both online and offline channels. In addition, the brand created awareness through billboards in major markets.

Over a period, as Zomato became an established brand, it created interesting partnerships with several brands having high user traffic. For instance, to make the ordering experience simpler, Zomato partnered with popular maps platforms such as Apple Maps and Google maps. These partnerships let customers book a table right within maps through Zomato. To make the payment experience smoother, Zomato partnered with popular mobile wallet players like Paytm to provide in-app cashless payment experiences. To reach out to users travelling to new places, Zomato partnered with travel sites like MakeMyTrip to provide restaurant-related content. It also partnered with many banks to provide interesting offers on the use of their credit cards. Through these kinds of partnerships, Zomato increased its brand visibility, content consumption and transactions at multiple touchpoints.

Combine knowledge of market with the power of technology

Technology not only helps in running the business efficiently, but it is also very valuable in drawing new audiences and creating new markets. Zomato has always been on the forefront of technology and has utilised it to innovate, create differentiation, stay ahead of competition and attract new users.

Zomato has made itself more attractive for advertisers, looking to reach the niche target segment at the perfect time by providing hyperlocal advertising options. If a user comes from a particular locality and is looking for certain types of food options, advertisements are shown for local restaurants providing the desired cuisines. This targeted advertising using technology created a significant impact on businesses of restaurants leading to the popularity of Zomato as an advertising platform.

In 2011, smartphones had just started becoming popular in India. To reach out to the user base accessing internet through their smartphones, Zomato became one of the first Indian companies to launch its apps for all major mobile operating systems such as Android, iOS, BlackBerry OS, Nokia OVi, Windows, etc. Initially, 80 per cent of the users would access the website and only 20 per cent of the users would access the app, but now more than 80 per cent of the users access Zomato through its apps and mobile site.

To adapt to different markets, Zomato customised the platform according to the needs of the local markets and made the product available in several languages other than English, such as Italian, Spanish, Portuguese, Turkish, Polish, Indonesian, Brazilian and Slovak. Moreover, there are a vast number of food habits in different markets. For instance, in the Middle East, users look for halaal food, in Western markets they look for vegan and organic food and in India they look for veg and non-veg options. To meet the needs of users in different markets, Zomato localised its product using different filters and features for different markets.

Along with making its product fast, efficient, adaptable and scalable, the team has also focused on making it collaborative. When Zomato entered new markets, to adapt to these markets and beat the competition, the team developed many customised features within the product. At a few places, Zomato acquired the competitor and integrated their localised business models and interesting features with its product. For example, MenuMania, Zomato's first acquisition in New Zealand, had a map-based search feature that is now available on Zomato everywhere. Similarly, Lunchtime, an acquisition in Czech Republic, had a strong business model around lunch menus, which, too, was integrated into Zomato.

By keeping one foot in the market and the other in technology, Zomato has been able to seize growth opportunities quickly and has been able to adapt its product to meet its customers' needs.

Jack Welch has said, 'An organization's ability to learn and translate that learning into action rapidly, is the ultimate competitive advantage.' Zomato's journey is a testament to this statement. The founders of Zomato didn't have a background in the food and restaurant industry, but they identified a problem and kept on learning from the market.

DEEPINDER GOYAL

When Zomato entered new markets, its teams didn't know much about the culture and food habits of these markets, but they learnt, unlearnt and relearnt many things. By translating these learnings into actions quickly, Zomato has been able to sustain its competitive advantage and has become an inspiring technology leader, an unbeatable competitor, an innovative company and an iconic brand.

Advice from Deepinder Goyal

- First create a niche and then execute well to expand it. But during expansion, don't lose focus of your core offering.
- Keep your business basics strong. If your base is strong, you can move fast and win.
- Look for advice and learn from the success and failures of others. But keep in mind that every startup is different and the journey of anyone else can't be copied as it is. Markets, employees, competition, customers, etc. of other startups could be different from yours. So, filter out a lot of stuff and see what works for you and what does not.
- In the world of technology, things change very quickly and there can be many possible versions of the future. Instead of creating a five-year plan, create a six-month plan, achieve it and then plan for the next six months.
- You must constantly be in the learning mode and you can never get to a point where you believe that you know it all.

Turning Mumbai's street food into a national fast food

Burger, pizza and coffee are commoditised products, but entrepreneurs like Ray Kroc, Tom Monaghan and Howard Schultz created unique business opportunities around these products and built world-class brands—McDonald's, Domino's Pizza and Starbucks respectively. What Ray Kroc did with burger, Tom Monaghan did with pizza and Howard Schultz did with coffee, Venkatesh Iyer is doing with vada pav.

Vada pav is one of the most popular street foods in Mumbai. Venkatesh Iyer, co-founder and CEO of Goli Vada Pav, has taken this humble fast food from the streets of Mumbai to other Indian cities. Starting with a single store in 2004 outside Kalyan railway station, near Mumbai, Goli Vada Pav is now India's largest ethnic fast-food chain with over 300 stores in 100 cities across 20 states of India. By December 2017, the company was selling more than 1 lakh vada pavs everyday through its owned and franchised outlets.

Goli Vada Pav has been covered as a case study at some of the world's top business schools such as Harvard Business School, IMD Switzerland and ISB Hyderabad. The company has won numerous awards, including the Coca-Cola Golden Spoon Award, for being the most admired fast-food chain of Indian origin. Moreover, *Travel + Leisure*, an international travel magazine owned and published by Time Inc., has featured Goli Vada Pav amongst the top 20 QSR brands in the world. In 2013, one of India's leading research agencies rated Goli Vada Pav as the sixth largest fast-food company in India. Interestingly, the first five slots were occupied by international brands like Domino's Pizza, McDonald's, Pizza Hut, KFC and Subway.

This chapter covers the inspiring journey of Goli Vada Pav, one of the most recognised Indian brands in the highly commoditised fast-food industry.

THE BEGINNING OF THE JOURNEY

Venkatesh Iyer was born in a middle-class Tamil-Brahmin family. Like in every middle-class family, his parents wanted him to study well and become an engineer, a doctor or a chartered accountant, or get an MBA degree and work in some big multinational company. He was an average student, and he was often told at home:'If you don't study well, you will end up selling vada pavs.' No one, including Venkatesh, had ever imagined that one day he would become the world's most popular vada pav-wala.

Disappointing many people around him, Venkatesh managed to graduate from Mumbai University with a BCom degree. Fortunately, he got a job in a financial services firm. After working with a few similar firms, in 1996, he founded his own small boutique financial services firm. His work involved organising funds for businesses from banks and other sources. He witnessed some really big-ticket deals and received handsome fees. This was the time when he had an office in South Mumbai and a chauffeur-driven luxury car. His family was happy to see that things were working out for him. But Venkatesh had other thoughts.

After working for more than 15 years in the financial services sector, the life of black suits, silk ties, closing deals and signing contracts stopped giving him a sense of achievement. He started having the urge to do something different. Something through which he could impact the life of a common man. This was also the time when Venkatesh's life was occupied with international brands starting from Colgate for toothpaste, Gillette for razors, Levis for jeans, Rayban for sunglasses to Blackberry for mobile, Compaq for computers and so on. While using these global brands, he always thought of creating an Indian brand of global stature that could become a part of people's daily consumption and could enable him to create jobs for the masses. But he was not sure of the industry.

When one of his friends, who worked as a senior executive in a global food company then, said in frustration, 'No matter what you do, Indians will eat Indian food only!' Venkatesh sensed an opportunity. It made him think of entering the food industry, but he was not sure of the product.

Food is a vast subject with multiple varieties. Being Tamil, the first product that came to Venkatesh's mind was idli, then came dosa, followed by biryani and sandwiches. Surprisingly, vada pav didn't strike his mind initially. One afternoon, Venkatesh arrived near Mumbai's Chhatrapati Shivaji Terminus for a meeting. He was hungry and he bought vada pav from a roadside vendor. After walking a few steps, he noticed a 30 feet wide McDonald's banner hanging from a building, announcing the opening of the restaurant in that location.

He looked at the burger on the banner and the vada pav in his hand and found that both the products were similar; if the burger had a patty, mayonnaise and lettuce between the bun, then the vada pav had a vada, chutney and chilli between the pav. One was non-spicy, the other was spicy. He instantly visualised these two fast-food products as near identical twins. An idea crossed his mind: if McDonald's can become one of the world's largest fast-food companies by selling burgers, then why couldn't a fast-food chain be created around its lookalike—the vada pav. Being a Mumbaikar, Venkatesh had eaten countless vada pavs since childhood, but he now saw it differently. He thought that the vada pav's status could be upgraded, so that it could stand along with the burger.

BIRTH OF THE BRAND NAME: GOLI VADA PAV

Goli is a commonly used word in Mumbai lingo. When Venkatesh shared his plan of leaving finance and starting a vada pav business no one believed him. After listening to his plan, people used to say '*Kya goli de raha hae!*' (You must be bluffing!) He got this response from almost everyone he shared his idea with.

He was determined and reached out to his contacts in advertising agencies to suggest a brand name for his vada pav business. Many people advised him to keep an English name. He wanted to start an Indian brand, so the suggestion of keeping an English name didn't work for him. He looked up to Indian food brands like Haldiram's and Chennai's super-famous Murugan's Idli, and thought that these brands would not have been that powerful if they had been called Sam's Bhujia or Peter's Idli. As he was getting into the street food business, he wanted to come up with a name that connected with Mumbai's streets, spirit, ethos and contours.

In Mumbai, the round raw potato patty is called 'goli', which after being dipped into a gram flour mix and fried becomes 'vada'. One day, he was having a conversation with his co-founder Shivadas Menon about the number of 'golis' prepared by a few of the leading vada pav vendors daily. This discussion was heard by one of his friends, who curiously asked him, what goli he was talking about repeatedly. Venkatesh told him that the round raw potato patty is called 'goli'. Suddenly, the name 'Goli' clicked for everyone in the room. The name was directly linked with Mumbai's lingo and the product. Therefore, the team decided to call the brand 'Goli Vada Pav'.

BUSINESS LESSONS

There are many important business lessons that can be learnt from the evolution of Goli Vada Pav. A few of them are as follows.

To make it big, understand every small aspect of your business

When Venkatesh was considering starting a business in the food industry, he began analysing every small aspect of the business to move in the right direction. A cost-benefit analysis made him realise that while 50 masala dosas or 50 sandwiches couldn't be served in five minutes, 50 vada pavs could be served in that time. Moreover, while plates and spoons were needed while serving food items like idlis and dosas, vada pavs could easily be carried and eaten on the move. Since people don't necessarily need to sit down to eat a vada pav, Venkatesh could save on real-estate costs, which would have otherwise been a major expense.

To evaluate market demand, instead of looking at the vada pav as a finished product, he looked at its ingredients separately. He found that though vada pav was very popular in Mumbai, its ingredients were popular all over India. Vada is made from potato, which is eaten in almost every part of India and is a key ingredient in all popular snacks such as dosas, samosas and aloo parathas. Another important ingredient of vada pav is besan (gram flour). Besan is also eaten in almost every part of India and is a key ingredient in popular snacks such as pakora, bhujia and dhokla. Vada pav has spices, and Indians are known for their love of spices. Another component, pav, is made of bread, which is also well loved across the country. He felt that because of the acceptability and the popularity of its ingredients across India, he could take the combined form—vada pav—to a national level.

From an alternative analysis perspective, he found hygiene to be a common element that was often missing in street food. He saw a huge opportunity to differentiate by selling vada pav in a hygienic manner. He found that international brands often found space required for expansion to be a challenge. For instance, McDonald's stores needed approximately 3,000 sq. ft or more real estate, air conditioning, seating space, etc. Due to location constraints and finance requirements, McDonald's stores could not be opened anywhere, unlike vada pav stores that required just around 300 sq. ft and no air conditioning or seating space. He realised that by selling hygienic fast-food, he could serve the segment that didn't have access to brands like McDonald's.

To imagine his revenue opportunity, Venkatesh did some mental calculations. At that time, India's population was around 100 crores. He felt that if he could reach at least 50 per cent of the population, that is, 50 crore people and make them eat one vada pav worth ₹10 even once in a year, his annual revenue could reach ₹500 crores. He dreamt further and thought that if 50 per cent of the population ate his vada pav 10 times a year, then his revenue could reach ₹5,000 crores.

An opportunity analysis from multiple aspects increased his confidence to enter the vada pav business.

Brand-building starts from operations

Many people think that brand-building is about painting stores, giving uniforms to the staff, putting nice banners and boards. But these front-end aspects are not helpful until a product or service provides a consistent experience to its customers. People prefer to buy a branded product or service because they get consistent quality and experience. For providing consistent brand experience, all back-end operations must run very well.

The most important aspect of food is taste. To keep the taste consistent, Venkatesh planned to invest in a centralised kitchen where raw golis would be prepared and supplied to outlets. His team tried countless variations of the goli by altering the masalas and other ingredients. After multiple experiments that went on for months, eventually the team finalised a recipe and decided to take it to the market. After setting up the kitchen, the next target was to set up stores. Venkatesh bought a second-hand Maruti van to transport golis from the kitchen to the stores.

In early 2004, the first store was opened near Kalyan railway station, which is one of the busiest suburban stations near Mumbai. The Goli store was different from the other vada pav stores in terms of colours, branding and hygiene. Moreover, the vada pavs were wrapped and the staff was well dressed. Venkatesh wanted to attract passengers from the railway station to his vada pav store, but there were many other stores in the same lane and it seemed difficult to drive footfall towards the Goli store. Venkatesh was not sure which marketing idea would work to get people's attention as people were busy listening to train-related announcements.

Suddenly, an idea clicked in his mind. He went to the person making the train announcements and told him that a small boy Tunnu couldn't find his parents and had been standing for some time at the Goli Vada Pav store. The train announcer made a few announcements for Tunnu's parents to pick up their son from Goli Vada Pav. These announcements caught the attention of thousands of people at the railway station. Within a few minutes, Goli Vada Pav became a known name. From that day, the Goli Vada Pav store became a meeting point for people. Soon, Goli's vada pav became famous for its taste and hygiene, and franchise inquiries started coming in.

By the end of 2005, Goli Vada Pav became a chain with 20 stores, of which three were company-owned and the remaining 17 were franchise stores in Kalyan and nearby areas. Venkatesh was happy to see that his model was working, but then he found a few gaps in the operations. The golis being prepared in the centralised kitchen had a shelf life of only 10–12 hours, so the ones being supplied to stores in the morning would turn stale by late evening. Every day, nearly 3,000 golis were being wasted. Venkatesh also got to know about pilferage. A few franchises used to pull out a small quantity of material from the original golis and create extra golis to increase their profits. This led to smaller vadas at a few of the stores. Another problem arrived when the chef went on vacation. A new chef made some changes in the masala mix and the taste of the vada pav changed.

Venkatesh realised that unless he could ensure uniformity in taste and consistency in quality standards, he couldn't establish Goli Vada Pav as a brand. Another issue was that the prices of the ingredients were not static so whenever prices of, say, potato or onion went up, his margins would go down. Even with increases in the demand for the product, franchise inquiries and sales numbers, the business was not making profits due to operational challenges. The business that had expanded quickly till 2005 started looking unviable in 2006.

Venkatesh wondered, if he couldn't manage 20 stores all within 20 km of each other, how could McDonald's manage thousands of stores globally. To find a solution to his problems related to standardisation, pilferage and taste, he met many people from the food industry and tried many experiments, but nothing worked. All his experiments failed and he lost a lot of money. One day, an acquaintance said, 'Venky, vada pav will not become a burger, but you will surely become a beggar!'

But miracles happen. Eventually, he came across Vista Processed Foods, the sole supplier of burger patties to McDonald's in India. Venkatesh partnered with them and started manufacturing his raw vada pav golis in their world-class automated plant. This partnership became the foundation of standardised back-end operations and the growth of Goli Vada Pav.

Design your startup to scale up

The way designs of cars and airplanes play an important role in defining their speed, the design of a business plays an important role in how quickly it can scale up. Goli Vada Pav is a one-of-its-kind modular organisation that has divided its business model into different modules and then has designed interfaces to correctly link all the modules. The company has outsourced much of its supply chain and operations, and it focuses on assembling the outcome of all parts into the finished product and then supplying it to its franchises. This business design has led to cost savings by reducing their fixed expenses.

Though the partnership with Vista solved the problems of wastage, pilferage and non-standardisation, a new problem came up. To increase the shelf life, the vadas manufactured in Vista's plant were frozen, and frying these frozen vadas required a different kind of fryer. The fryers used by McDonald's were extremely expensive and buying them for multiple stores would have made Goli's business model unviable. Venkatesh decided to create his own chip-based automatic fryer at an affordable cost. He convinced two of his friends who had a technical background and another friend who was a software programmer to help him in inventing an automated fryer for frying frozen vadas. Eventually, the 'Goli fryer' was invented at a much lower cost compared to the fryers used by McDonald's.

Since vada pav masala has, among other spices, a strong colouring ingredient in turmeric, Vista informed Goli that they wouldn't be able to prepare the masala. As a solution, Venkatesh converted Goli's previous kitchen into a vada pav masala 'formula plant'. Now Venkatesh had to solve another problem: the frozen food logistics network used by McDonald's was not affordable for Goli. So, he reached out to Jeena & Company, an end-to-end logistics operator for the food industry. Jeena & Company used to transport items like ice creams, bakery products, vegetables, milk products, etc. Venkatesh shared his requirement with their representative, and fortunately the company agreed to provide frozen logistics and cold storage support to Goli Vada Pav.

Finally, to store frozen vadas at franchise stores, Venkatesh needed a refrigerator that could give a stable $-18°$ centigrade temperature. He discovered that assembled deep-freezers used by restaurants could give up to $-5°$ centigrade temperature. After a lot of research, one day, he learnt that ice cream refrigerators at grocery stores could meet the required temperature. For pavs, the Goli team partnered with selective local bakeries. He had found every component to stabilise Goli's supply chain.

By setting up this process, Goli has been able to serve vada pavs even in the remotest areas of India. Using back-end tracking mechanism, the Goli team coordinates the whole process and if any complaint comes from any franchise, the fault can be tracked to any link of the supply chain from the delivery van to a box to a packet to the field from where the raw potato was procured.

Larry Ellison has said, 'If you do everything that everyone else does in business, you're going to lose. The only way to really be ahead, is to "be different"'. The fact that Goli Vada Pav became India's first vada pav company designed with external partnerships and a modular structure is a testament to Ellison's words. This business design has been helpful in accelerating the expansion of Goli Vada Pav.

The product is the same—the humble vada pav—but with the use of technology, logistics and franchising, it has become a national fast food. Prestigious business school IMD Switzerland did a case study on Goli Vada Pav and defined it as a 'hollow organisation', which means an organisation that grows by retaining only a few of its components in-house and choosing to develop through outside support.

When one door closes, look for a new one

Alexander Graham Bell said, 'When one door closes, another opens, but we often look so long and so regretfully upon the closed door that we do not see the one which has opened for us.'

Though Venkatesh had managed to create a popular vada pav brand in the Mumbai suburbs and a strong back-end to support his business, he was not left with any money to scale up his business. He needed a few crores for business expansion, but he didn't have anything left to mortgage, so he zeroed down on the equity route and decided to raise funds from an angel investor.

The vada pav business was seen as a low-end business, so he thought that if a person of high reputation invested in his business, his company would get noticed by the world. He began his groundwork by scanning profiles of all the top Indian corporates. During this search, he got to know about Jerry Rao, who had been the CEO of a foreign bank in India and then founder of an extremely successful BPO company. He was well known and highly respected in the industry. Venkatesh tried getting in touch with him but learnt that he had moved overseas. Somehow, Venkatesh was able to find his oversees number and called this number every morning (midnight for Jerry Rao) for a span of a year. Though Venkatesh couldn't speak with him, he left a voice message every day. Parallelly, he was actively looking for funding from other sources, but he couldn't get the attention of investors, who were focusing on sectors like IT and BPO at that time.

Though Venkatesh was persistently trying to raise funds, he was upset because of his numerous failed attempts. At one of his meetings, he met a journalist and shared his story with him. The journalist found Goli's story interesting and asked Venkatesh to look at the next day's newspaper. The next day, Goli was featured in *The Times of India*. In the meantime, NDTV was doing a story on Mumbai food and heard about Goli Vada Pav. Soon Goli Vada Pav was on TV. From there on, the brand came to be mentioned in many media articles.

One fine day, Venkatesh got a call from his former boss, who was an investment banker. He told him that Jerry Rao wanted to see Venkatesh. Eventually, Rao invested in Goli Vada Pav, and a few more reputed angel investors followed. Along with the investment came the responsibility of scaling up the business. From the supply chain side, Goli Vada Pav was ready, but to expand the number of stores the company needed real estate in various parts of Mumbai. The team faced multiple challenges: the cost of renting real estate in Mumbai was very high compared to the suburban areas; people preferred renting small shops to ATMs and grocery stores and felt that a vada pav store would spoil the ambience; and big spaces were already in demand by retail chains, hence not available for a brand like Goli Vada Pav. The Goli team tried various options but nothing seemed feasible from cost, location and store size points of view.

As they were struggling for real estate, Venkatesh noticed Aarey Milk Booths that were present across the city, on footpaths, on major roads, in major areas. The Goli team shortlisted 300 locations from 1,500 where Aarey Milk Booths were present and partnered with Aarey. Now, Goli Vada Pav was present in co-branded stores at all major locations in Mumbai, including Nariman Point, Peddar Road, Gateway of India, Juhu beach area and Bandra sea-face. Venkatesh saw his dream of setting up a national brand progressing and he was excited.

Unfortunately, his excitement turned into a nightmare. Somehow, without his knowledge, vada pav became a politically sensitive topic in Mumbai. Maybe because of its high visibility in Mumbai, Goli Vada Pav found itself amid a turmoil for all the wrong reasons. Goli's team started getting threats and extortion calls along with unreasonable demands by the booth operators' union and so on. One day, one of the existing stores was burnt and Venkatesh decided to exit the Aarey partnership. By this time, he had used up all the funding in setting up fryers, refrigerators, branding and logistics for these 300 stores. His adventure became a misadventure with a lot of negative publicity. His father said, 'I have never seen someone burn 4 crores in 4 months.'

Venkatesh thought that he could raise more funds from the market, but then came the news of the collapse of Lehman Brothers. With one of the world's largest investment banks filing for bankruptcy in 2008, all the money evaporated from the market. Despite this, Venkatesh found a few investors who believed in the India growth story. He was close to raising funds, but then the Satyam and Subhiksha fiascos happened in 2009. The discovery of the massive accounting fraud at the IT company Satyam and the closure of the Indian retail company Subhiksha due to financial mismanagement shook the confidence of investors in Indian businesses. A lot of deals went on hold or were terminated, including Goli Vada Pav's funding deal.

Venkatesh was in a deep crisis and was not sure how to take his business ahead. Then one fine day, a man based in Nasik, who had tried Goli's vada pav at its Kalyan store, called to inquire about opening a franchise in Nasik. This was the start of a new chapter in Goli Vada Pav's growth story. When all the doors seemed to be closed, a new door was opening.

Create your comeback

Martin Luther King, Jr once said, 'If you can't fly then run, if you can't run then walk, if you can't walk then crawl, but whatever you do, you have to keep moving forward.'

After the Aarey fiasco, Goli Vada Pav's stores faced a crisis as most of the existing franchises in Mumbai suburb became reluctant to continue. This franchise inquiry from Nasik was a ray of hope. The first store in Nasik was a very different kind of experience for the Goli team. In Mumbai, vada pav is a commodity but in Nasik, people saw it as Mumbai's famous fast food coming to their city. People liked the product and Goli Vada Pav became a popular brand in Nasik. Word of mouth travelled to Aurangabad, and a few stores opened in the region. Soon, Goli Vada Pav expanded to various regions of Maharashtra, and within the span of a year and a half it had opened close to 75 stores outside Mumbai. During this expansion, Goli trained multiple bakeries across Maharashtra to prepare Mumbai-style pav.

Though Goli was rapidly expanding in the interiors of the state, its presence in Mumbai and its suburbs had become negligible. People in Mumbai and the corporate world thought that the fastest growing vada pav brand of Mumbai had disappeared. Then an interesting thing happened. TiE (The Indus Entrepreneurs) was organising an entrepreneurship conference in Mumbai. Venkatesh thought of taking up a stall at the conference to serve vada pavs. He was not aware of the scale of this conference, but he was aware that many leaders of corporate India would visit the conference. To his surprise, this conference turned out to be one of the largest entrepreneurship conferences in Asia with more than 2,000 participants, including iconic speakers like Ratan Tata, Narayana Murthy and Kishore Biyani.

In this conference, Venkatesh also got an opportunity to speak in one of the sessions and the combined effect of his inspiring talk, the taste of vada pav and the enterprising nature of his team, Goli Vada Pav became one of the most talked about brands at the conference. Many stalwarts visited Goli's stall and enjoyed delicious vada pavs. One among these stalwarts went on to become a future investor—Sarath Naru, the founder and managing partner of Ventureast, one of India's leading venture capital funds. This journey from almost getting closed in Mumbai to becoming the largest vada pav chain in Maharashtra was a strong comeback for Goli.

Marketing can happen without megabucks

Many people think that marketing always needs money. But Goli has been known for building its brand using innovative methods.

One day, Venkatesh met a film producer from the Marathi film industry and asked him how he was going to market his latest movie. All the answers that the producer gave required a lot of money. Venkatesh told him about Goli's presence in the state and informed him that every day thousands of people visited Goli's stores. He suggested putting up the movie's posters in these stores. The producer agreed and in exchange promised to show Goli Vada Pav in the movie. A Goli branded bus-stop was created and showed in two shots in the movie, and movie posters got visibility across all Goli stores. Later, similar barter deals were done for many other Marathi movies.

Following Maharashtra, Goli expanded to South India across the states of Karnataka, Andhra Pradesh (now Telangana and Andhra Pradesh), Tamil Nadu and Kerala. Venkatesh was happy to see that the vada pav was getting along with idlis and dosas and people were enjoying it as another interesting fast food. Later, Goli expanded to North India across states such as Madhya Pradesh, Uttar Pradesh, Chhattisgarh, Punjab, New Delhi and Haryana. Then, it expanded to the eastern states such as West Bengal, Orissa, Jharkhand and Bihar followed by western states such as Gujarat.

Initially, Goli had only three varieties of vada pavs, but as it expanded across various states, to meet the taste requirement of people in various regions of India, the company added many new spicy and non-spicy vada pav varieties to its menu. Later, many other fast-food items that used vadas and pavs were added to the menu. These new products were much liked by customers and word of mouth brought in more footfall to the stores. Interestingly, the media also wrote articles on vada pavs being available outside Maharashtra.

To keep the customers engaged, Goli's team came up with a few more interesting ideas. The team thought that since the vada pav is Mumbai's product, people should get a feel of Mumbai while eating it. The team went to Kalyan railway station and recorded announcements of train services such as '*Platform number 5 par aane wali local ab platform number 8 par aayegi*'. The way dine-in restaurants play soothing music, Goli's stores played the sounds of Mumbai's railway stations. People who were from Mumbai but were working in various other cities liked these recordings and brought many of their friends to the stores to show them how it felt to be at stations in Mumbai. Interestingly, one day a customer at a Goli Vada Pav store uttered a famous dialogue from the most famous Bollywood villain—Gabbar Singh from *Sholay*. In Gabbar's style, the customer said to his friend: '*Tune burger, pizza bahut khaya … ab "Goli' khaa!*" A store boy repeated the dialogue, and looking at him a few other customers copied it too. Soon, this dialogue spread like wildfire across the city.

One day, the Goli team found Balvir Chand, a lookalike of legendary cricketer Sachin Tendulkar. Balvir is also a great mimicry artist. He can sing, talk and entertain a crowd. Balvir joined the Goli team and became a face to create excitement and draw people's attention during store launches and other BTL (below-the-line) activities. On the day of the launch of a new store, Balvir's posters are put up in small cities and he travels in an open jeep waving to the people and greeting them. During the inauguration, he drives a large crowd to the new store and interacts with the visitors, giving them autographs and taking pictures.

To connect with the youth, Goli became an active brand on Facebook. The company created a Facebook page—'Vadapav + Cutting Chai + Amchi Mumbai = Awesomeness'. This page has three categories: 'Goli Gyan', 'Garam Goli' and 'Goli Gossip'. The team regularly posts stories in these categories, which get a lot of engagement from followers in the form of likes, shares and comments. Venkatesh also started his own blog called 'Vada Pav Murmurings'.

Starting with his first talk at the TiE Mumbai Summit, Venkatesh has given more than 300 talks at various business conferences and educational institutes including Harvard Business School, IMD Switzerland and ISB Hyderabad. A few years ago, he wrote a book titled *My Journey with Vada Pav*, which became one of the most popular books about entrepreneurship and was well received by the corporate world as well as general readers. Along with many other initiatives, Venkatesh's talks and his book have played an instrumental role in making Goli Vada Pav one of the most recognised Indian fast-food brands.

Along with expanding its business, Goli Vada Pav is actively working towards making a social impact at the bottom of the pyramid through employment and entrepreneurship opportunities for farmers at the back end and store boys at the front end. As Goli Vada Pav is scaling up, more opportunities are getting created for people.

Jeff Bezos once said, 'The common question that gets asked in business is, "Why?" That's a good question, but an equally valid question is, "Why not?".' The journey of Goli Vada Pav is a testament to this statement. When the whole world was questioning Venkatesh's decision to get into the vada pav business, he was thinking about why the vada pav couldn't be branded like the burger. Eventually, he created a national fast-food brand through the vada pav. He is optimistic that, like the world has embraced the American burger and Italian pizza, one day it will also embrace India's vada pav.

VENKATESH IYER

Advice from Venkatesh Iyer

- Technology is a differentiator for any business. To become a game-changer, explore how technology can be applied to every aspect of your business. The technology of automated plants gave Goli Vada Pav a strong foundation to scale up the business and digital technologies like Google Search made it possible for people across the globe to find content on Goli.

- Imagination and exploration are very important traits of entrepreneurship. Through imagination, an entrepreneur can think beyond defined limits and boundaries, and through exploration, they can find new solutions that were not thought of by others in the past.

- A brand is not viewed in isolation, it is viewed along with its associations. In isolation, Goli was a company selling a street-food item. But its association with reputable investors, institutions, partners, awards and the media changed people's perception and helped it become a reputable brand.

- Money is not the only means to enable marketing. Apply creativity and explore barter opportunities to create visibility for your brand.

Making learning better for millions of students

India is a young country with nearly half of its population under the age of 25. If this young population gets access to proper education it could contribute not only to the growth of India but also to the growth of the whole world.

While there is a lot of focus on education in India, challenges like access to quality teachers are yet to be addressed. As a solution to this problem, the culture of private coaching classes has emerged across the country. These classes supplement education at schools. But as the good private coaching classes gain popularity, the number of students increases, which brings us back to the same issue—the lack of personal attention to an individual student. Additionally, in many small towns and villages, good private tutors are not available.

Students are under tremendous pressure to perform well in exams. With marks being considered an indicator of their learning, students focus on memorising rather than understanding concepts. Rote learning not only means that one soon forgets what they memorised, it also takes out the fun involved in real learning.

When there are challenges, entrepreneurs create opportunities to make an impact. One such entrepreneur is Byju Raveendran, whose company BYJU'S has revolutionised the way students learn.

Today, BYJU'S is India's largest education-technology (ed-tech) company that is trying to help millions of students learn better through the internet. In 2015, for the K–12 segment, BYJU'S launched its flagship product—BYJU'S The Learning App. The app went on to become India's most popular learning app. As of December 2017, this app had 12 million downloads and 7,00,000 paid users.

According to media reports, BYJU'S received significant rounds of funding from investors like Tencent, Verlinvest, the Chan Zuckerberg Initiative (CZI), IFC, Sofina, Sequoia Capital, Lightspeed Ventures, Aarin Capital and Times Internet.

This chapter covers the journey of BYJU'S, a brand focused on making learning better for millions of students.

THE BEGINNING

Byju Raveendran grew up in a small village in Kerala in southern India. He had a keen interest in mathematics and science, and he learnt these subjects by asking questions about why and how certain things happen. After his schooling, he studied mechanical engineering at a government college and in 2001, he joined a shipping firm as a service engineer.

In 2003, Byju visited Bangalore for a vacation when a few of his friends were preparing for the Common Admission Test (CAT), the entrance examination for the Indian Institutes of Management (IIMs). He helped his friends in their preparation by sharing his techniques and strategies. Though not planned, thanks to his friends' suggestion, he also ended up sitting for the exam. Four of his friends passed the exam and Byju scored in the 100th percentile. He became the CAT topper. In fall 2005, he helped more friends prepare for CAT. He also took the exam again and once again scored in the 100th percentile and became the CAT topper for the second time. He realised that there was something different about his approach towards the exam.

Even after topping CAT twice, Byju didn't do an MBA. He never intended to start an education business either, he just wanted to pursue his passion for teaching.

BIRTH OF THE BRAND NAME: BYJU'S

In 2006, Byju quit his job as an engineer and took up teaching full-time. He started offering CAT preparation classes called Byju's Classes for CAT. He started small with around 35 to 40 students, mainly his friends, whom he started teaching at coffee shops. Slowly, as the word of mouth about his teaching strategies started spreading, his students started getting more students, who then, brought in more students. Within a few weeks, the class size grew to approximately 2,000 students and Byju had to rent an auditorium to hold classes. Byju's popularity kept on growing and students kept on coming due to word of mouth. Later, auditoriums also became inadequate and to accommodate students, he booked stadiums as well. Eventually, he realised that he couldn't keep on accommodating new students continuously and had to adapt to technology to scale up.

Also, while teaching, Byju noticed that there was a huge gap in the way students learn and how concepts can be learnt. He felt that to make a real impact on the way students learn and to make them fall in love with learning, he should reach out to them during their school years.

In 2011, Byju formed a new company—BYJU'S. The motivation behind this was to venture into the K–12 segment, that represents school-going students from kindergarten to the 12th grade. Since Byju's Classes had already become a very successful brand, Byju decided not to lose the existing brand popularity. He just moved from Byju's Classes to BYJU'S.

BUSINESS LESSONS

There are many important business lessons that can be learnt from the evolution of the brand BYJU'S. A few of them are as follows.

Experience your consumers' world

To really know about your consumers' challenges, it is important for you to experience their world and empathise with them. Looking at things from a consumers' perspective can help you enhance your product or service. Byju has always tried experiencing the world of his students, initially by himself, thereafter along with his team and now through technology. Based on the insights gained, the BYJU'S team has adapted quickly to come up with better ways to help students.

While scaling up his classes, Byju carefully observed his students' reactions, performance and challenges and introduced many new approaches to make learning fun for his students. When his company, BYJU'S, entered the K–12 market, he enrolled students into multiple tutoring centres in Bangalore. Each centre gave BYJU'S teachers an opportunity to interact with students. Through these sessions, teachers understood the reaction and questions of school students.

To engage a school student, the learning module needs to be simple, engaging and effective. The BYJU'S team worked on creating a format that would make learning so interesting that students would start learning on their own. They noticed that some students liked to learn through stories, some liked to see visuals and some liked to learn the actual theory. So, they incorporated all three approaches to adapt to each learning style.

To meet the requirements of different types of students, the BYJU'S team focused on personalising learning for each student using data science and big data analytics. The team categorised the content, learning, assessment and practice modules. By integrating assessments with videos, teachers were able to identify areas where students struggled. Then they mapped each wrong answer to a specific learning gap and recommended targeted remedial videos and activities. These videos have been made more engaging by using techniques like virtual reality and gaming.

After four years of intensive research and development, in July 2015, BYJU'S launched its app for the K–12 segment. This mobile app uses a mix of video lessons and interactive tools to personalise learning for students across grades and geographies. To take learning to a whole new level, the company has leveraged big data analytics to trace the learning fingerprint of every student and has created a personalised learning experience on its platform. The app is personalised to the style, size and pace of learning of each student. By transforming the one-to-many generalised learning model to one-on-one personalised learning experiences, this app has set a benchmark in education technology nationally as well as globally.

Become your biggest competition

When you are creating a new category and market segment, you can't rely much on analogies and case studies, so it is important to compete with yourself and keep on becoming better rather than resting on early achievements. The success of a brand in one segment facilitates its entry into related segments leading to market expansion.

Though education is a mature market, our education system has several challenges such as lack of quality school teachers, similar teaching approach for all students, and learning being driven by the fear of exams and not by the love for learning. Though many private coaching classes and online tutoring platforms have been around for decades, many of them adopt a rote-memorisation approach rather than encouraging children to learn on their own. Through its new approach, BYJU'S has created a new category in the education industry—a visual and engaging platform that helps students learn better and encourages them to learn on their own. To make students start learning on their own, the BYJU'S approach focuses on instilling the love for learning in students. It is creating a new segment of students who are becoming self-paced learners with their parents and teachers taking up supporting roles. Through a unique combination of content, media and technology in every learning programme, BYJU'S has been able to make learning effective, engaging and personalised.

Though the approach adopted by BJYU's has been unique and effective, by competing with itself the company has been pushing itself to continuously innovate and come up with better ways to refine its approach for various segments of students. The company's first market segment was CAT aspirants. In 2006, Byju used to take personal classes for CAT in Bangalore. As his popularity grew, he started travelling to multiple cities. With demand continuing to grow, Byju decided to scale up using technologies like videos and VSAT. By 2010, with the help of technology, Byju was reaching out to students in 92 locations.

While teaching CAT aspirants, Byju realised that to really make a difference in the way children learn, it is extremely critical to help children learn better right from their formative years. Hence the K–12 product was started. Starting with small batches of students from 8th to 12th grade, he then entered the 6th to 8th grade segment followed by 4th to 6th grade segment. For every subject, the BYJU'S team developed around 100 hours of content and four to five different styles of videos to explain every concept. After four years of intensive research and development, BYJU'S had built content for six grades and was ready to launch its digital product. In 2015, BYJU'S The Learning App was launched for the K–12 segment. This app has become a platform to make quality learning experiences more accessible.

In early 2017, the company launched the BYJU'S math app for 4th and 5th grade students. The application has been designed to offer younger children a platform to explore the world of math through games, interactive videos and quizzes. This app merges appealing features of game design and technology with innovative and rich interactive videos from India's best teachers who teach abstract math concepts visually and contextually. This app makes the whole process of learning mathematics easier as well as helps students understand how it is applied and used in real life. Use of teachers with technology as an enabler makes the delivery of the concepts easy, effective and engaging.

To provide better learning experience to students, BYJU'S is continuously innovating its product by focusing on various areas of content, media and technology. On the content front, the team extensively researches a topic to determine what to teach the students. Then, suitable and interesting metaphors are identified to help students understand key concepts. For every script, key elements such as engagement questions, sticky metaphors, visual elements, common misconceptions, frequently asked questions and some elements of humour are identified and included in the script.

On the media front, the team converts the finalised script into a second-by-second storyboard. The storyboard serves as a base to create the final video lesson. It also helps teachers understand what they would need to explain in the video and in what sequence. Next, the teachers record the lesson. In the post-production stage, the media team adds an appropriate background and multiple layers of artwork such as 2D animations, 3D animations, simulations and virtual objects.

On the technology front, a rich learning profile is built for each student. This enables the app to customise and personalise the learning experience for everyone based on their strengths and weaknesses along with their specific learning gaps, pace and needs. The BYJU'S personalisation engine is powered by deep knowledge graphs of over 50,000 concepts and relationships. Additionally, the learning content is also tagged to multiple other properties and parameters at the sub-micro concept level and this helps the algorithms create a smooth learning curve for students so that they feel challenged yet motivated. Whenever they make a mistake, the app identifies the right remedial method to strengthen their learning experience. This is similar to how a personal tutor would try and tackle his students' gap in learning, but it is more effective since it has deep insights. Additionally, BYJU'S analytics systems capture millions of data points every day. This drives multiple decisions from improving a feature to building highly contextual recommendations. The variety of student profiles also gives the company an idea on what to improve or add to the overall content and overall user experience.

There is a fine difference between a consumer and a customer. Consumers use products while customers buy them.

Sometimes they are the same person, sometimes not. In the case of BYJU'S, students are the consumers of the app but parents are the customers. The parents pay for the subscription. Additionally, they encourage their child's learning journey as participative stakeholders. Along with experiencing the world of students, BYJU'S empathises with parents and has a companion app for them. Generally, for parents, the assessment is limited to test and exam reports. There is no deep understanding. Through this app, parents can understand the areas where their child is putting in effort, observe where the gaps are and provide pointers for specific areas.

By competing with itself, BYJU'S is constantly renewing its competitive advantage and making it extremely difficult for external competitors to match its total value. Byju says, 'We are our biggest competition and our focus is to outplay ourselves every time with new innovations which make learning more fun.'

Build a great team

Having a team that truly feels and understands the brand is a necessary ingredient for success. The team at BYJU'S is focused on just one thing—getting students addicted to learning. The strong core team has been organically built and all the core team members have been in the system for over eight years. All of them have a unified mission—to create the best learning experience for students globally.

BYJU'S has been extremely selective about the quality of teachers. The company strongly believes that the role of a teacher is more of a 'performer' than just delivering a lesson the conventional way. It is essential that a teacher has great content knowledge, good delivery, enthusiasm, passion to teach and a strong screen presence to deliver the lesson in a format which students like and can relate to. BYJU'S initial set of teachers were handpicked by Byju from amongst his students. Today, BYJU'S has more than 120 teachers who research every concept to ensure it is explained well in every session for students to understand, and out of those 120 teachers, only 14 of them act in the learning videos.

The company has a robust R&D team of more than 600 people across media, content and technology that continuously works towards creating the best learning products. The content team comprises engineering graduates who have excelled at college and other examinations, subject researchers, and seasoned teachers with 10–15 years of experience. The media team has a mix of technology experts and creative people such as 3D designers, visual-effects specialists and musicians. These team members not only understand the 'what' but also the 'how' and 'why' of learning. The company has an in-house band that creates the music for the videos. The technology team has some of the best minds with experience in the fields of gaming, education and IT. This unique blend of expertise reflects in the brainstorming of ideas and the one-of-a-kind learning programmes created at BYJU'S.

In 2017, the BYJU'S family, across all departments, grew from 1,200 to 2,000 BYJUites across the country. The company has a flat organisational structure, where BYJUites can express their opinions directly to the senior leadership. Also, internal communications play a very important role at BYJU'S. Regular updates and internal events on various occasions help in establishing a bond among team members.

Redefine the boundaries of your market

For many new categories, markets are small to begin with. But with new ideas, product modifications, new distribution channels, different price points and marketing campaigns, entrepreneurs find new ways to expand the market.

BYJU'S started with a very small market. Initially, Byju used to teach his friends at coffee shops. Quickly word of mouth spread and the class size went up from 35 students to 100 students in classrooms to more than 2,000 students in auditoriums to 20,000 in stadiums.

To cater to working professionals, workshops were organised in auditoriums on weekends where the first session was free and was followed by paid sessions. Students came to these workshops to get trained by a CAT topper. Each session was like a performance where large 20x16 screens displayed the content, while Byju stood in the background. Quickly Byju became very popular on employee forums at technology companies.

As his popularity grew, Byju expanded to four cities. On weekends, he ran workshops in Bangalore, Chennai, Mumbai and Pune. In 2007, Byju started targeting undergraduate students in five new cities. He started doing workshops for 150–250 students in college campuses on weekdays.

In 2009, with demand continuing to grow, Byju decided to expand by using videos. He created video lessons using a tablet PC. Every Sunday he conducted a live session in Bangalore and on the subsequent weekdays, he streamed the video recording to the centres in other cities. To manage growth, Byju convinced a few of his students to join his team. His team went around the country to identify colleges where students were interested in enrolling for Byju's sessions and created centres. He launched online video-based learning for CAT through VSAT and, without compromising on quality, reached out to 92 centres across the country. These sessions were a huge success.

In 2011, Byju decided to enter the K–12 segment. He conducted workshops for 8th to 12th grade students, offering the first session for free. Many students from these workshops joined BYJU'S centres in Bangalore. In 2015, BYJU'S The Learning App was launched for the school-going segment.

From starting with a few students at a small coffee shop in Bangalore, by December 2017, BYJU'S had reached 12 million students across the country, and it is now extending its reach to students in international markets as well.

Turn your consumers into your brand advocates

A consumer is someone who uses your product, but a brand advocate is someone who goes a step beyond and actively tells others about your brand. Word of mouth is the most powerful and trustworthy form of communication. Students talk to students, parents talk to parents, students and parents talk to each other and so on.

Byju's focus has always been on helping his students rather than selling a product. He started his teaching journey by helping a few of his friends in their CAT preparation. His friends loved his way of teaching and started bringing more friends and did a lot of word-of-mouth marketing for him. Later, when he started teaching more formally, he would take free sessions for students. With increased demand, Byju saw thousands of students enrolling as well as paying for his sessions.

The BYJU'S app follows a 'freemium' model, where students get access to the content for free for about 15 days, post which they can subscribe for advanced levels at different price packages. With an average time of 53 minutes being spent by a student on the app every day, the app has become the most loved and preferred education app for students across age groups.

To build a successful brand, it is important to think about your positioning. This helps determine how differently you are perceived from your competition. When many of its competitors focus on preparing students just for exams, the focus of BYJU'S has been on developing students' love for learning so that they become self-paced learners. Following the positioning, it is important to consistently communicate who you are and what you stand for. Any form of communication, whether public relations or advertising, cannot take place in silos. The main message of BYJU'S has always been about 'falling in love with learning'. Also, in every message, BYJU'S targets only the end users, that is, the students. All its marketing campaigns have a good mix of different channels like print, television and digital.

To create brand awareness among students and parents, the company launched a student-centric TV advertisement alongside a digital campaign on various social media platforms. The social media campaign targeted urban students while the television commercials aimed to reach rural students with limited internet access. To increase the visibility of the television commercials, both children- and parent-centric television channels and show timings were targeted.

The app received a great response with millions of downloads. The sales team of BYJU'S categorised these downloads based on usage, paid subscription and so on. Many of the users opted for paid subscription after using the free version. In many cases, the sales team educated parents about the usefulness of the app and shared data about their child's app usage. The validation of the app's effectiveness is the renewal rate of 90 per cent year on year. In fact, 70 per cent of the students on the app are from outside the top ten cities.

Over a period, many marquee investors have invested in BYJU'S. This funding has helped in accelerating product development, hiring new team members and market development. In 2016, the Chan Zuckerberg Initiative (CZI), a philanthropic initiative of Facebook founder Mark Zuckerberg and his wife Priscilla Chan, invested in BYJU'S. Mark Zuckerberg's Facebook post announcing the investment got 1 million likes. BYJU'S also received a lot of press coverage across different Indian states and its app's overall organic downloads increased leading to more usage and more advocacy.

As of December 2017, the app had 12 million downloads and 7,00,000 paid users, and the number has been increasing exponentially month by month. The app has become the world's largest school learning app.

BYJU'S approach has paid huge dividends, many of its consumers have become its brand advocates and through their word of mouth have made it one of the most popular education brands in India.

Byju says, 'Success to me is making an impact. Today, we have not even reached out to 1 per cent of the total school-going population. There is still a long way to go before we call this a learning revolution. The real impact will be when we get millions and millions of students learning right from their formative years at school.'

Moving forward, to make an impact in the global education system, BYJU'S is expanding its footprint in international markets, especially the English-speaking markets. It is working on developing learning programmes for more grades and more subjects, and modifying its product as per the context and learning style of students across geographies.

BYJU RAVEENDRAN
2×2=4

Advice from Byju Raveendran

- There is no particular time when one should start. If your idea is addressing a need and you have a strong model backing it—that is enough. Obviously, it is also important that you are passionate about the idea and love doing it.
- Always capitalise on your strengths! This helped me to think big and transform something that started in coffee shops to a global learning app. Overall, if you are passionate about your idea, be persistent and work hard for it from the beginning.

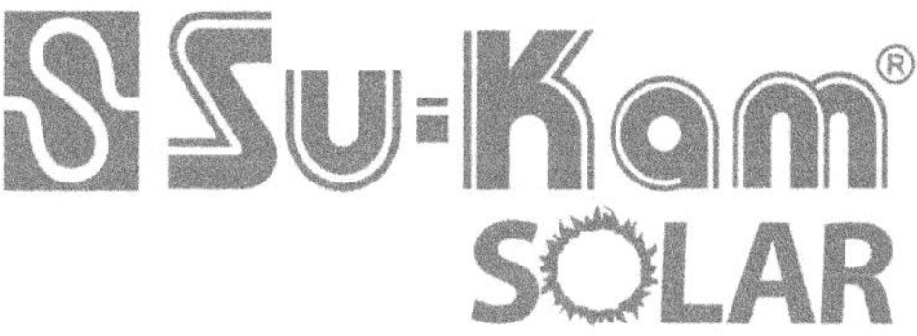

Making electricity accessible
and affordable

What comes to your mind when you think of electricity? Is it Thomas Edison, the person who invented the light bulb? Or is it modern electrical appliances such as refrigerators, TVs and air conditioners? Can you imagine life without electricity? It is tough, right?

The hard fact is that billions of people on this planet still don't have access to electricity and even if they do, the supply isn't adequate or reliable. Power shortages are frequent and the duration of these shortages is also long. In the absence of electricity, electric bulbs can't be lighted, children can't study, factories can't operate, workers can't work, electrical appliances can't operate and even mobile phones can't be charged. This results in substantial losses for the economy.

This sorry state of electricity shortage has continued for generations, because either the power backup solutions were not available or in limited supply if available, and they were either unaffordable or unreliable. Then came into the picture a game-changer with a non-technical background, who with his hard work and determination created affordable and reliable solutions for the masses.

Kunwer Sachdev, the poster boy of India's power backup industry, is the man behind Su-Kam Power Systems. Su-Kam has been recognised as one of the fastest-growing and most innovative organisations in India. The company provides power backup solutions such as solar inverters, batteries, UPS, home inverters, solar panels and other solar products for both retail and institutional customers. In 2003, Su-Kam became the first company in India's power backup industry to start exporting power backup products and solutions to foreign markets. Today, the company has operations in 90 countries worldwide with close to 50,000 channel partners. In 2013-14, Su-Kam recorded revenues of ₹1,200 crore.

This chapter covers the journey of Su-Kam, the first Indian power solutions company to win the title of 'Superbrand', which is considered the 'Oscars of Branding'.

THE BEGINNING

A true rags-to-riches hero, Kunwer Sachdev was born and raised in Delhi's Punjabi Bagh area in a lower-middle-class family. As a railway clerk, his father had a meagre salary. Additionally, his father always wanted to run his own business, so he would invest a portion of his salary in trying out small businesses, none of which succeeded.

Kunwer studied in a Hindi-medium government school and from a very early age, he learnt that it takes a lot of hard work to make money. During his childhood, along with his brother, he used to sell ball pens on a bicycle. He grew up with a dream to start his own business someday. In 1984, he graduated from college and joined his brother's stationary shop full time. He was always full of ideas and sometimes even became a source of laughter and ire for his family and friends. He pushed his brother to start their own brand Su-Kam for pens, but his brother was not comfortable with Kunwer's nature of dreaming big. In a few years' time, Kunwer started feeling that he couldn't work with his brother. He decided to make something of his own and this created tension within the family. No one would have thought then, that someday Kunwer would establish himself as a successful businessman. But he did.

Initially, for around two years, he worked as a sales executive in a cable TV company and earned around three to four thousand rupees per month. In 1989, with his savings of ₹10,000, he started his own cable TV installation business named Su-Kam Communications. In 1992, he started manufacturing cable TV accessories. By 1998, his manufacturing business had a turnover of ₹3 crores to ₹4 crores. This growth gave him the confidence to think bigger, and he started thinking about the next big opportunity.

During those days, power shortages were a major problem in various parts of Delhi so Kunwer bought an inverter to use at home. Sadly, this inverter gave trouble frequently and Kunwer would end up calling the electrician every other day. One day, he got so frustrated that he decided to open the inverter and look for the problem. Inside the inverter, he found a sub-standard PCB board and a dirty mesh of wires. He took that inverter to his factory and, along with his R&D team, analysed it. The team spent a good amount of time looking at the quality of inverters present in the market and were shocked to find that all the inverters available in the Indian market were built with poor-quality parts with nearly no technology. Kunwer even got inverters from Canada to look at the working of a sophisticated product.

Being a visionary, he was quick to foresee the opportunity in the power backup industry. Power shortage was an immense problem, available inverters were of poor quality and foreign products were not suitable to cope with a wide range of fluctuations in markets like India. He decided to shut down his cable TV business in 1998 to start Su-Kam Power Systems.

THE BRAND NAME: SU-KAM

Interestingly, Kunwer Sachdev has named all his businesses so far Su-Kam. You would be curious to know the story behind the name. Sometimes a brand name reflects one's feelings. Su-Kam is a true testament to that.

Back in 1982, when Kunwer was studying at Hindu College, Delhi University, he liked a girl and wanted to marry her. In fact, he had also thought about the names of their future kids.

This was the period when Kunwer was thinking of starting his own business producing pens. The name he thought for his business combined the initial characters from the girl's name, his name and the names of their future children. He originally thought of the brand name Su-Kan in which 'Su' came from the first two letters of the girl's name, 'K' came from his own name, and 'a' and 'n' were to be the first alphabets in the names of his future kids. He hired a designer to get a logo designed for the brand name Su-Kan, but the designer mistakenly changed the last letter 'n' to 'm' and delivered a logo for Su-Kam. Kunwer had already paid the designer ₹450 for logo design and didn't have more money to get the name corrected. Interestingly, he liked the name Su-Kam and decided to go ahead with it.

Things didn't work out between Kunwer and that girl, and they decided to move on. Even though the reason behind the name had lost its significance, Kunwer had liked the brand name Su-Kam and so he retained it.

BUSINESS LESSONS

There are several important business lessons that can be learnt from the evolution of Su-Kam in the power systems space.

Don't lose faith in yourself

George Bernard Shaw once said, 'Don't lose faith. Promise yourself that you will be a success story, and I promise you that all the forces of the universe will unite to come to your aid; you might not feel today or for a while, but the longer you wait the bigger the prize.' Kunwer's journey is a testament to this saying.

Though he used to sell pens on a bicycle, Kunwer's childhood dream was to become a doctor. He had cleared his medical entrance exam but lost admission because he got only 49 per cent in his class XII board exams while the eligibility criteria for admission to a medical college was 50 per cent. He repeated class XII and topped in his school, but this time he could not clear the medical entrance. Due to a stressful financial situation, he didn't have the option to try once again. He could get admission into an engineering college, but he was not interested in engineering. So, he enrolled for a BA in Mathematical Statistics at the prestigious Hindu College. He dreamt of starting his own brand of pens, but as his aspirations didn't match his brother's and he didn't want to compete with his brother, he decided to stay away from the pens business.

To manage his finances, he took up a day job in a cable TV company, and he attended law college in the evenings. Though

Kunwer was determined and wanted to do something big in life, he was not sure how he could make things happen for himself. Working for someone else as an employee didn't excite him, so he thought of starting his own business.

But he needed money for that. He didn't have rich parents or properties to mortgage. He faced many difficulties in raising funds on his own. There were times when he was unable to pay back the lenders on the designated date, but he never tried to escape from the situation. He faced his lenders and requested for extensions, which he always tried to meet.

When he entered the cable TV business, he was good at sales, but he did not know anything about manufacturing, the installation process and technology. Initially, he faced a hard time meeting his customers' expectations. Once a customer even locked him in a room and didn't let him out until Kunwer repaired his cable. His failures and hard times made him determined to learn technology on his own. As he started understanding business and technology, his business started doing well. To make something bigger, he switched his focus and entered the inverter manufacturing business. The first 100 inverters were returned by buyers because of glitches.

He kept on improving his inverters and eventually developed better products than anyone else in the Indian market. Initially, he started selling inverters directly to customers. He turned many of his cable TV business customers into his inverter business customers. He also reached out to many new customers by cold calling. He realised that he couldn't scale up his business by selling directly to customers. Instead, he had to cultivate dealers and distributors, as they ensured a wider geographical coverage and provided professional support to customers, thereby resulting in greater demand and, consequently, increased sales.

During this period, the market was very crowded. There were many small inverter manufacturers who were selling poor-quality products. Kunwer thought of consolidating the market and converting these manufacturers into Su-Kam's dealers. But no one was interested in becoming Su-Kam's dealer, so Kunwer started giving his inverters as samples to prospective dealers to try out for a few months.

In a few months, some manufacturers realised that they couldn't match Su-Kam in terms of product quality and price. They accepted Kunwer's offer and became the company's dealers. Slowly, word of mouth about Su-Kam's innovations, product quality and competitive pricing started spreading. Over the years, many small inverter manufacturers all over India turned into Su-Kam's dealers. Simultaneously, he also converted battery dealers into Su-Kam's distributors. There was no looking back and, with time, Su-Kam entered many other related businesses like batteries, UPS, solar-based products, etc.

Su-Kam became the first company in the industry to start exporting its products to foreign markets. Kunwer travelled around the world to identify opportunities and develop products for new markets. As he entered new countries, he faced new challenges around government policies, business norms, local laws, competition, etc. But along with his team, Kunwer overcame all the challenges and established Su-Kam as a leading brand in many countries.

Under Kunwer's leadership, Su-Kam's rise in the power backup industry has been extraordinary. Its products have given a tough time to competitors not only in terms of quality, but also pricing. For achieving remarkable success in his entrepreneurial venture, Kunwer Sachdev has received numerous awards and recognitions including the Bharat Shiromani Award by the Government of India and the Entrepreneur of the Year by Ernst and Young.

Turn problems into opportunities

Many people accept problems as they are, but very few convert problems into opportunities. Kunwer is one of those few. His entry in the power backup industry started from a problem at his home, where a locally purchased inverter couldn't sustain frequent power cuts. Because he had been in the cable TV business, he had a fair idea of electric and electronic systems. He opened his inverter, and within the mess of wires he saw a huge opportunity.

Power shortages had been a major problem in India. In a way, many businesses, factories and households couldn't operate efficiently because of power shortages and voltage fluctuations. Additionally, inverters available in the market were of poor quality and unreliable. During this period, generators were very popular, but they were expensive, noisy, and cumbersome to operate. Kunwer turned this problematic situation into a huge business opportunity by developing low-cost, reliable and mass-marketed power backup solutions, which he kept on improving.

By looking at problems of various businesses, Su-Kam developed many customised solutions for them. For example, many petrol pumps need to operate 24x7, and sudden power failure leads to loss of fuel, the time and money of the customers as well as the petrol pump owners. Moreover, power sources like diesel generators have a higher switching time leading to a shutdown of the dispenser pump. To solve these problems, Su-Kam developed an inverter that ensures that petrol pumps don't face any power interruption.

The lack of adequate power supply in the remote locations of Assam and neighbouring states like Manipur and Nagaland was another issue, as it increased the dependence of the Indian Army on cumbersome sources of power backup such as diesel. Su-Kam worked in unison with the government authorities to become the largest provider of solar-powered backup solutions in Northeast India. The solar power plants installed at remote locations in this region are being used to fulfil the daily energy needs of offices and residences of Indian Army's Assam Rifles team. The use of solar energy is also contributing to a greener environment.

There are lakhs of households in the remote villages of India that never had electricity. Su-Kam has explored the huge market of bringing electricity to rural areas. It led its first-of-its-kind solar project with the Uttar Pradesh government and installed solar DC System in over 40,000 households in the remote villages of UP. These households now have electricity 24x7. Su-Kam also executed a similar project with the Tamil Nadu government and installed solar home lighting in 27,000 houses in the state.

In the absence of electricity, life used to come to a standstill after sunset in many African villages. If electricity is available after sunset, small businesses can thrive, students can study and people can engage in various social activities. Su-Kam installed solar street lights in many of these villages. Now people in these villages have access to both electricity and employment.

Kunwer entered the power backup industry with a few lakhs of personal savings, but with his knack for identifying problems that can be converted into business opportunities, he has been able to create a business with a turnover of more than ₹1,000 crores.

Cannibalise your existing products

Steve Jobs famously said, 'If you don't cannibalise yourself, someone else will.' Employing a similar philosophy, instead of getting satisfied with the success of his previous products,

Kunwer continuously pushes his team for new innovations and cannibalises his own products.

Before Su-Kam's entry, the inverter industry was dominated by hundreds of local players who were selling substandard products. But Kunwer's entry challenged the entire industry and changed it for the better. He wanted to develop high-quality inverters in India, but at the time he couldn't find good people within the industry. So, he started looking for people across different industries such as UPS, digital products, automobile and missile.

Su-Kam became the first company in the industry to invest in and institute a separate R&D unit, which is certified by the Department of Scientific & Industrial Research (DSIR), Government of India. Besides leading the overall business of the company, Kunwer also heads Su-Kam's R&D division. Since its inception, this R&D unit has come up with many world-class innovations.

In 2000, Su-Kam revolutionalised the inverter market by replacing transistor-based inverters with MOSFET-based inverters. The company made India's first MOSFET-based inverter, which was one-fourth the size of the traditional inverter and had much lower cost and much better efficiency. Moreover, traditional inverters used to run on two batteries, but Su-Kam's inverter used only one. In 2001, Su-Kam launched India's first sine wave inverter. Before this innovation, all inverters used to run on traditional technology of square wave and used to fail due to rampant power fluctuations. But the sine wave inverter worked well even when there were rampant power fluctuations, thereby protecting sensitive appliances. Moreover, it didn't have that irritating humming sound. In 2002, Su-Kam launched the world's first plastic body inverter, which was much lighter and more visually appealing than the traditional metal body inverters.

This plastic inverter was judged as the innovation of the decade by India Today. In 2003, the company came up with the world's first Home UPS system, which integrated two separate power backup devices—the inverter and UPS. This system eradicated the need to buy a separate UPS for a computer. Later, Su-Kam made India's first inverter that could sense outside temperature and automatically regulate the charging current and voltage of batteries. The list of Su-Kam's innovations is endless and owing to his many contributions to the industry, Kunwer is also known as the 'Inverter Man of India'.

Kunwer has revolutionised not only the inverter industry but also other areas within the power backup industry, such as UPS, batteries and solar-based products. He is particularly interested in making green energy, that is, solar energy, available to everyone in India, to suit the needs of all, from a small house in a remote village to big industries. To name a few of its innovations in the solar industry, Su-Kam has developed India's first touchscreen and Wi-Fi–enabled solar power conditioning unit, which can be monitored from anywhere in the world through a laptop, tablet or phone. As another example, the company has created a DC system, which comes with LED lights and fans, and runs on pure DC generated by solar panels leading to no conversion losses. Kunwer's efforts have helped Su-Kam acquire the largest market share in the solar residential sector in India. Because of his contribution to the solar industry, Kunwer is also recognised as the 'Solar Man of India'.

Interestingly, Su-Kam is not just a pioneer in hardware innovations, it has also created many innovative softwares for monitoring and diagnosing problems in power backup products. The company has a portfolio of more than 250 products and has developed power backup solution for almost every industry. Su-Kam is credited with filing the largest number of patents in the industry. It holds a record for being the only company in its field to file for over 100 patents, and it continues to file nearly two technology patents every month.

Get inside people's minds

The starting point of brand development is to get inside people's minds and make them think about your brand. Kunwer has never stopped thinking differently and has made sure that Su-Kam's branding is present at all high-visibility places.

Kunwer knew billboards were a good medium for brand awareness, but the cost of billboard advertising was too high. So, he devised a clever solution; he partnered with dhabas to put up signboards. Dhabas are roadside restaurants in India that are usually found on highways and on the outskirts of cities and villages. They not only serve food but also act as stopping points for truck drivers, tourist busses and people passing by on the highways.

Kunwer made boards with the name of the dhabas and printed Su-Kam underneath them. This was a win-win situation for both the dhaba owner and Su-Kam as dhabas got a signboard and Su-Kam got visibility. Starting in the year 2000 with dhaba owners in Haryana, he later covered Punjab, UP and then all of India. Interestingly, at many places dhaba owners paid him for these boards. This exercise gave the brand Su-Kam high visibility and high recall at minimal cost. This smart marketing strategy was later adopted by many other brands as well.

Kunwer found many other high-visibility and low-cost advertising options. When he visited the Dal Lake in Srinagar, one of the most popular tourist places in India, he saw many beautiful shikara boats. Soon, he got all these boats covered with Su-Kam branding. Later, he got Su-Kam's branding done on traffic barricades. He also launched vans with Su-Kam branding that acted as mobile power sources and carried a 100 KW inverter to supply power.

Before Su-Kam's entry in the power solutions industry, no company had proper marketing collaterals of products, but Kunwer changed that norm by coming up with creative marketing collaterals for all products from Su-Kam. Su-Kam is considered the first inverter brand to advertise in newspapers. In this case too, Kunwer thought differently. He realised that a regular half page ad in a newspaper cost much more than the combined cost of classified columns covering half a page. Instead of buying half a page of ad space, he started buying classified columns together covering half a page of the newspapers. Later, many newspapers changed their classified ads policies because of him.

Su-Kam launched the first-of-its-kind business-themed TV reality show in the country called *Sales ka Baazigar*, which became a large platform to identify enterprising salespersons. The show was open for participation for anyone within the age group of 21–30 years and the minimum qualification was 10th class matriculation. An eminent panel of judges shortlisted the best candidates at each stage. The top ten finalists from the show were absorbed by Su-Kam at attractive pay packages. The show got an amazing reception. Thousands of people participated, some coming even from remote villages, and millions of people watched the show on their TV screens.

Kunwer is also famous for being an exceptional orator. He has been one of the most sought-after speakers at many eminent conferences. His simple and interesting way of talking helps him make a direct connection with the audience. The popularity of his talks has also played an important role in establishing Su-Kam's brand.

Take care of your employees and partners

Kunwer believes that brand experience first starts internally and then spreads externally. Happy and knowledgeable employees can improve customers' experiences leading to the development of brand trust. Everyone who works with Su-Kam feels proud to be a part of the organisation. The organisation focuses on the development of its employees through various trainings and professional development programmes. It also creates new challenges for employees to upgrade their skills. In addition to all this, the company organises many initiatives to increase bonding among employees and with the company. It celebrates all festivals in full spirit. Moreover, it encourages employees to take care of their health by organising an annual sports week.

Like employees, Kunwer considers his channel partners (dealers and distributors) as extended family and regularly organises channel partner meets. In these meets, Kunwer and his team focus on understanding and answering the queries of the channel partners and educating them on new technologies and products. Unlike channel partner meets of many other businesses, Su-Kam focuses only on educating partners, not on sales. Partners are not asked to bring any cheques or make any purchase commitments in these meets. In a year, Su-Kam organises more than 200 channel partner meets in India and abroad.

To make sure that learning of both employees and channel partners is consistent, the Su-Kam team has created videos for every solution. Many of the solution videos are used by the sales team and channel partners while meeting customers and are shared on YouTube for an audience interested in learning about new-age power backup solutions.

Su-Kam has a nationwide network of thousands of service engineers and customer care executives who work day and night to ensure that their customer's problems are resolved quickly. The company has developed many digital solutions to help its employees and channel partners work more efficiently. These digital solutions help employees in syncronising their work and help the company monitor their progress. The company has developed a mobile application for its distributors that helps them control their billing with dealers and track inventory.

Su-Kam has won more than 50 awards for its groundbreaking innovations, corporate excellence and talent management.

Thomas Edison invented the light bulb. Like him, there are a few other entrepreneurs who can claim to have impacted the way the masses experience the power of electricity. Kunwer Sachdev is one of them. His inventions have earned him a place in the business world as an entrepreneur who not only founded one of the most admired Indian brands, Su-Kam, but also revolutionised the power backup industry.

KUNWER SACHDEV
Electricity

Advice from Kunwer Sachdev

- Knowledge of the English language may help you in getting good academic scores in college, but in the market, local languages can help you in getting more positive outcomes when compared to English. Don't ignore the power of local languages.

- Stay modest throughout your life. Sometimes, when people become successful and known, they ignore modesty and show arrogance. Arrogance may satisfy the ego but it spoils relationships.

- The dynamics of running a 5 crore business are different from those of running a 50 crore and a 500 crore business. When a business is small, it is agile like a horse, but when it becomes big, it gets slow like an elephant. As a business evolves, it becomes important to evolve your systems and processes, and evolve yourself as a leader in terms of your business and people skills.

When we were schoolgoing kids, we all heard the story of David and Goliath. A young boy David defeated a giant warrior Goliath. Because of this memorable and inspiring win of little David over giant Goliath, people use the David and Goliath analogy whenever a small player defeats a big one. In this chapter, we will explore another version of the story of David and Goliath.

From a business perspective, let's consider David to be a small startup and Goliath the market leader. David is fast, flexible, innovative and a risk taker. Goliath has resources, money, brand name, customers, and systems and processes to manage a large-scale business. In the first version of the story, David was able to defeat Goliath because, looking at his own strengths, Goliath became complacent and didn't think that David would attack him with an out-of-the-box strategy. What would have been the outcome of the story, if Goliath would have thought and responded like David? Goliath would have been undefeatable.

This story is about FirstCry, a brand that started as a David and evolved into a Goliath in its industry, but still ideates and executes like a David.

FirstCry was founded in late 2010 in a Pune-based row house. By the time FirstCry decided to enter the baby and kids category, the category had already attracted many other specialised players. This included online players such as Babyoye.com and Hushbabies.com, and offline players such as the Mahindra & Mahindra group's Mom and Me. Around the same time, in the US market, acquisition of Quidsi, Inc., operator of Diapers.com, by Amazon for around $ 545 million made this category attractive for many other competitors. Over a period, horizontal e-commerce players like Amazon and Flipkart also entered this category and the market became hyper-competitive.

Many of the niche players in this space have either shut shop, got acquired or are struggling to survive. There was a time when Mom and Me and BabyOye used to be the strongest and largest niche competitors of FirstCry but at some point they merged and later, FirstCry acquired this combined entity. Today, FirstCry is India's largest omni-channel (web, mobile and offline) retailer focused on the needs of babies, kids and mothers. It also runs India's largest maternity clinic gift hamper programme, offline stores chain and online parenting communities targeted towards parents. Moreover, it also started a logistics business called Xpressbees, which has emerged as one of India's fastest growing logistics companies.

According to media reports, FirstCry has received significant funding from investors like SAIF Partners, IDG Ventures, Valiant Capital, the Switzerland-based private equity fund Adveq, Singapore's Temasek Holdings-backed Vertex Ventures, NEA, Mahindra Group, Infosys co-founder Kris Gopalakrishnan and

Tata Sons' chairman emeritus Ratan Tata. Moreover, along with a few of these investors, Alibaba has also invested in Xpressbees.

THE BEGINNING OF THE JOURNEY

In 2001, Supam Maheshwari, co-founder and CEO of FirstCry, was blessed with a baby girl. At that time, he used to run Brainvisa Technologies, an eLearning company, and his work required him to travel to the US and Europe often. He would bring back a lot of products for his daughter because many of them were not available locally.

As he began researching, he figured that the baby and kids' products industry in India was a multibillion-dollar industry, but it was highly unorganised and extremely fragmented. Even though many customers had the spending capacity, they didn't have easy access to world-class brands or, for that matter, variety and quality products.

In 2007, Indecomm Global acquired Brainvisa. After leaving the company in 2009, Supam decided to create a platform that could give parents easy access to quality baby and kids products.

BIRTH OF THE BRAND NAME: FIRSTCRY

When a baby is in the mother's womb for nine months, it gets oxygen through the placenta that is attached to the mother. Once the baby is born, it is disconnected from the placenta and the baby's lungs take over the breathing. The baby's first cry acts as a kick-starter for its little lungs and is synonymous with breathing.

The first cry is the most precious and cheerful moment for parents. It is a joyous feeling for parents as they hear their baby say 'hello' to them and the world for the very first time.

Considering the importance of a first cry for parents, Supam felt that the brand name FirstCry would be a perfect fit. Fortunately, he found that the domain name Firstcry.com was available and he bought it.

In late 2010, along with his friend Amitava Saha, Supam started FirstCry.

BUSINESS LESSONS

There are many important business lessons that can be learnt from the evolution of FirstCry. A few of them are as follows.

Identify a niche market and become its leader

A niche market is a highly specialised market segment with customers having common characteristics and requirements. Startups have very limited resources and for them, niche markets are great places to begin as they have limited competition. Once a startup is successful in one segment, it can utilise its learnings and expand into other segments.

You may think that mass market players such as Amazon and Flipkart sell everything, then why are niche players needed in the market. Let's answer this with an analogy. The way a specialist doctor is valued more by patients than a generalist doctor, niche players are valued more by customers than mass market players. Mass market players sell products in multiple categories but focus on their top-selling categories. On the other hand, niche players focus on a particular category and provide huge depth, breadth and a specialised experience in that category.

Compared to many other players, FirstCry started small and late. However, from day one, the focus of the FirstCry team has been to provide the best experience to its customers. Though the vision was to cater to its market segment via both online and offline channels (through franchises), it started first with its e-commerce channel Firstcry.com. Initially, the company focused only on toys for metro-based, internet-using parents in the 25–35 age group with kids in the 0–2 age group. During the first month, Supam and his colleagues called up all their friends and family members within Pune and asked them to try the website. Serving these initial orders gave him a lot of learning about the packaging and delivery challenges of e-commerce businesses.

Supam realised that children's products are of different shapes and without proper packaging they could get damaged during transition. To understand packaging better, he ordered products from a few international websites and learnt about the materials and styles used for packaging various kinds of baby products. In parallel, he started establishing a supplier base, warehouse, logistics network, catalogue, etc.

With time, FirstCry expanded into product categories beyond toys and moved to age groups of -9 months (pregnant mothers) to 4 years, followed by 4 to 6 years. To reach out to India's continuously increasing smartphone users, the company launched its mobile app, which now contributes more than 70 per cent of online sales. The current portfolio of Firstcry.com includes more than 2 lakh products from over 2,000 top-notch national and international brands in every possible category and sub-category of products for babies and kids, in all price ranges. It has become the go-to destination for buying anything required for mothers, babies and kids during various stages of child development from -9 months to 6+ years. By aggregating demand and supply, FirstCry has made it possible for parents to buy any product for their babies and kids from the comfort of their homes. At the same time, along with many big brands, it has given visibility to many small brands that were developing niche products for this category and were spread across the country.

There is a huge customer base that is not comfortable with online transactions and prefers to touch and feel products before buying them. To reach this customer base, Supam planned to open offline stores especially in tier-2 and tier-3 towns, where real estate is cheaper, customers don't get preferred product choices easily and ecommerce penetration is not like it is in tier-1 cities. Though Supam's vision was great, execution was not easy. The skill sets required to operate an offline model are different from those required for an online model. This plan also needed to bring a synergy between the two ways of running the same business. Having no predecessors to look at for running both the online and offline model together, FirstCry's investors were apprehensive about this approach. They didn't want Supam to divert his focus and the limited resources of the company.

Supam convinced the investors that he would make sure that the offline channel didn't take away his focus and the company's limited resources. Instead of starting his own stores, he started franchise stores as franchise owners have local knowledge, invest their own money and, being entrepreneurs, give their 100 per cent in terms of time and effort. He started looking for like-minded partners who could share his vision and invest their own time and money. Fortunately, one of FirstCry's customers came forward and in June 2011, he opened FirstCry's first franchise store in a mall in Bharuch, Gujarat. The FirstCry team visited the store and helped in designing the interiors and setting up the store.

Later, to grow the franchise model, the company assigned one dedicated person to handle enquires and manage operations. By the end of the year 2011, five or six customers of FirstCry liked the opportunity and came forward to open franchise stores.

With time, the company streamlined the engine and scaled up the model. As of December 2017, FirstCry has over 320 franchise stores in 125 cities, and has five regional teams across the country to support its franchises.

As FirstCry started gaining knowledge of its customers' choices and preferences, it also started realising the gaps in products available in the market. There were many products that were available in international markets, but were not available in India. Also, many required products were not available in the required shape, size, variety and price range. To meet the unserved needs of parents, in 2013, FirstCry launched its private label brand—BabyHug. Today, BabyHug is trending towards becoming India's largest brand for products for babies and kids.

FirstCry has not only changed the way parents shop but also the way they connect. All parents have their unique experiences, challenges and questions around parenting. In the good old days, parents' networks were limited to friends, families, neighbours, colleagues and people in their phone book. However, using the power of the internet, FirstCry has started an online parenting community, enabling connections between parents who may not have met otherwise.

By thinking about everything a parent may need, FirstCry has not only created multiple business models but also the largest organised ecosystem for parents.

Increase speed and decrease costs

A few of the traits that separate winners from others include their ability to scale up, their focus on reducing costs and their agility. Focus on speed in all areas of business, such as ideation, decision-making, experimentation, execution and creating new competitive advantages, has helped FirstCry scale up fast. Their focus on low cash burn without compromising on quality has helped them do away with unwanted expenses. The company's core team is super focused on speed and low cash burn and has cultivated the same mindset within the organisation.

The core team observes its competitors' moves, researches secondary data, analyses customer feedback and listens to its investors, employees, vendors and franchises. Insights from all the sources help the core team members validate and refine their strategy continuously. Based on the experiments, the company identifies the processes and models that work and scale them up quickly. The models that don't work are either refined and retested or stopped. Supam says that there are two kinds of people within FirstCry—those who build new processes and others who use these processes and execute things mechanically. Both kinds of people continuously find ways to improve and make these processes more efficient.

The evolution of FirstCry's logistics business reflects this. A big part of customer loyalty is dependent on order fulfillment using efficient logistics. Initially, the company teamed up with third-party logistics partners to manage its customers' expectations of on-time and safe delivery of products. But with time, the team realised that this model of outsourcing deliveries to external partners was expensive and uncontrollable. FirstCry was not able to commit delivery timelines to its customers and it had no control over the last-mile customer experience. To overcome these challenges, in 2012 FirstCry started an in-house logistics division.

In parallel with external courier companies, this internal division started handling deliveries for both the online and the franchise business. Soon, this division grew from handling deliveries in a few cities to whole regions and then to multiple regions all over the country. With time, it started delivering orders for a few other e-commerce companies. Soon, this large division grew to become a separate business entity called Xpressbees. Over time, Xpressbees has become one of the leaders in the e-commerce logistics space, delivering more than 2,00,000 shipments every day—and this number is increasing exponentially. According to media reports, around the start of 2018, Alibaba, one of the biggest online commerce companies in the world, has invested in Xpressbees.

By scaling up both its online and offline businesses quickly, FirstCry has been able to create strong buying power. For many brands, it has moved from buying from distributors, to buying directly from manufacturers with better margins. Because of the expansion of its offline stores, the company has been able to distribute its inventory holding from backend warehouses to customer-facing retail stores. These stores have helped in increasing brand awareness, inventory offtake and sales. Moreover, the logistics costs in the franchise model are much lower as compared to online model, as orders in the case of the former are transported in bulk without any requirement of separate packaging for every item.

Become memorable among your target audience

Many businesses think short term and to gain their customers' mindshare, they keep on bombarding them with uninvited marketing messages, discounts and promotions. Their major focus is on somehow increasing the count of their customers and number of transactions. But a few businesses think long term and focus on continuously gaining their customers' love and respect. Over a period, they become memorable among their customers.

FirstCry has always focused on making memories that parents can cherish in the long run. As an example, to reach out to young parents, when they are celebrating the happiest moment of their lives at maternity hospitals, the company started the FirstCry Box programme. This direct-to-parents programme is a great opportunity for partner brands to share their product samples in the FirstCry Box. Along with sharing samples, partner brands also contribute to the programme cost. FirstCry packs products from various brands into gift boxes along with a high-value FirstCry gift coupon.

These gift boxes are delivered to hospitals based on the number of monthly baby births. Nurses gift these boxes to mothers within two days of the baby's birth. When parents get these gift boxes with samples of the items required during early days after birth, they feel connected with the brand's presents in the box and willingly fill feedback forms with their information such as their contact details and the baby's birth date. Using this data, FirstCry tracks and analyses the buying patterns of these parents on its website. FirstCry also remains in touch with these parents by sending weekly mailers covering relevant stories and up-to-date information on products they are likely to need in the immediate future. Moreover, these boxes create recall value in the long run because often mothers use these boxes to keep various baby items. As of December 2017, FirstCry had partnered with more than 10,000 hospitals in over 60 cities and was reaching out to around 1,50,000 new parents every month through its partnered hospitals. In other words, the FirstCry boxes were being gifted to over 2 million new parents every year.

This 100 per cent targeted programme has a lower customer acquisition cost and higher conversion rate as compared to other marketing models. At a very basic level, the programme has a customer acquisition cost that is almost one-tenth of an average TV campaign. In terms of conversion, around 25–30 per cent of the parents who've been gifted the box become FirstCry's regular customers. In terms of benefits for partner brands, a few of the brands have seen a fourfold increase in customers from amongst the parents compared to when they were not gifting. Many of them have been able to increase retail penetration of their newly launched products due to the demand generated in areas around the hospitals where the gifting happens. Because of impressive results, the FirstCry Box has become a preferred sampling channel for many established and emerging brands of baby products in India.

As another example, in 2015, the company started World of Moms, an exclusive community for moms by moms where they can ask as well as answer questions. This has become India's largest online community focused on motherhood. Additionally, in 2017, FirstCry launched another online community called FirstCry Parenting, which is open for both fathers and mothers. This community acts as a unique platform where researched parenting tips and tricks are shared in a manner that is easy to understand.

Through these communities, FirstCry has been able to remain in touch with parents for non-shopping reasons and has been able to improve the loyalty matrix. Both these communities are based on user-generated content. Their services are free for users who provide most of the content, and the business model is supported by advertising and partnership opportunities for various brands.

World of Moms has a lot of useful content such as stories, blogs and tips on child health, development and well-being. Moreover, it has over 500 recipes of baby food, information on the latest fashion trends and a classifieds directory that lists the best of education, art and coaching services and facilities in Indian towns and cities. Additionally, this community acts as a great platform for brands to get their new products tested and reviewed by moms.

FirstCry Parenting acts as a unique platform with information on the latest researched tips and tricks for parents such as more than 1,00,000 parenting FAQs, baby's shopping lists, baby's vaccination schedules, hospital checklists and so on. Moreover, this community has tie-ups with leading hospitals from where experts answer parenting-related queries.

After around five years of growth, though FirstCry had become popular among parents and had a customer repeat rate of over 80 per cent, the company noticed, through internal research, that FirstCry had low brand awareness. To increase its brand awareness and improve its brand identity, the company signed on Amitabh Bachchan as its brand ambassador. Bachchan brought huge credibility to the brand, due to his pan India appeal as one of the most adorable grandfatherly figures in the country. He has a huge social media following and connects well with FirstCry's target audience. The company made six TV commercials around the theme 'Bachchon ki shopping, bachchon ka khel nahi' and ran them across GECs, news and movie channels, along with outdoor, print, radio and digital support. To select the babies who would feature alongside the actor in the campaign, the company launched a digital marketing contest through its World of Moms community. This search brought a lot of traffic to the various properties of FirstCry.

Microanalysis facilitates mega success

Collection of the right data and its proper analysis provides answers to many important business questions. Data analysis not only gives information about areas that need immediate attention, but also keeps relevant stakeholders connected on business performance metrics. It also brings transparency and a sense of ownership among employees and helps in collaboration among various business functions for business planning. In a business like FirstCry, which has multiple marketing channels, business models, partners, hundreds of employees, thousands of suppliers and millions of customers, analytics play a very important role in driving decisions.

Along with its evolution, FirstCry has added many new channels in its marketing mix. Initially, the company focused on paid digital channels such as Google AdWords, Facebook ads, display advertising and referral sites. Over a period, the company has become active on many social media channels such as Facebook, Twitter, Instagram and YouTube. Moreover, it has been using email marketing for customer acquisition, retention, and for moving prospects to becoming customers. To increase its targeted reach and customer acquisition, the company has partnered with various players such as banks, travel portals, playschools, hospitals, catalogue players and stem cell companies.

With so many marketing channels available, figuring out which one to use, when and how much is a tough decision for the marketing team. The cost of marketing varies significantly, depending on the choice of channels. To decide which channel to use, when and how much, the company analyses the performance of every channel and every campaign independently for factors such as the number of customers acquired, customer-acquisition cost, customer lifetime value, payback period, etc. This analysis helps in replacing educated guesses with real data that is helpful in scaling up efforts on promising channels.

Every visitor to the website leaves their footprints. Growth in the number of customers also means that FirstCry now has access to significantly more amount of data related to buying patterns—preferences, unfulfilled requests, browsing history, repeat purchase rate, average order value, feedback, from where they came, etc. FirstCry uses analytics to gain valuable insights from this big data and fine-tune its products and offerings.

Understanding visitors' behaviours on its various platforms through various channels helps the company execute on identified areas and serve its customers better.

Along with marketing its offerings and getting orders, the company needs to manage a complex supply chain. It sources disparate inventories from multiple vendors in various cities. This inventory must be stored, packed, picked and delivered according to the customer orders at the right place, right time and in the right form and shape with proper packaging. As FirstCry runs multiple business models, such as the B2C business model through its online franchise partner who manages the consumer website, the B2B business through its franchise model, and sampling programmes like FirstCry Box, it needs to manage supplies from multiple vendors, warehouse operations, packaging and last mile logistics of multiple models in parallel. The number of SKUs sold through FirstCry is very high and many of them need special handling. To manage all the orders on time, a certain level of inventory needs to be maintained based on the periodicity of orders and the delivery cycles of vendors. At the same time, unsold inventory must be continuously tracked as it blocks money. With the help of well-defined systems and processes, and analytics to identify areas that need immediate attention and processes that need improvement, FirstCry has been able to build an efficient and productive back end.

Leverage technology to stay ahead

In today's digital era, technology is the backbone of any business. It helps a brand manage its experiences and relationships with both internal and external stakeholders. It touches every business area—right from being an interface for customers to browse and order products from, to being an enabler of back-end operations and transactions. Agility, scalability, security and availability are considered the basic deliverables for any company's technology backbone.

For the external world, FirstCry may be the biggest parenting brand in India, but internally it's a technology company that enables products to be sold through both online and offline channels, and connects parents with brands, specialist service providers and even each other. FirstCry has an in-house technology team that, along with managing the existing IT backbone, continuously experiments with new features and tests them. For example, the team developed India's first chatbot that can help parents in buying strollers by answering all their possible questions. Since FirstCry's franchise stores can only offer limited inventory as compared to the online store, the team has integrated its online and offline stores through 32-inch internet-enabled touchscreen kiosks at the franchise stores. Customers can choose any product from the online inventory through the kiosk and get the product delivered home.

From the perspective of an external audience, FirstCry serves its customers through multiple digital channels such as Firstcry.com, World of Moms, FirstCry Parenting, the mobile app and chatbots. Millions of customers visit these online properties 24x7 and look for information on products, price, availability and so on. Also, during in-house and partner marketing campaigns, traffic on its platforms shoots up drastically. From the front end, only interactive interfaces are visible, but at the back end, a lot of algorithms run to manage real-time responses and feedback systems, online ordering, product search, payment, personalised mailers, etc. Technology not only helps customers in effective decision-making, but also helps FirstCry manage its brand experience and relationships with customers by providing them the right information at the right time.

From the point of view of an internal audience, FirstCry has multiple internal functions such as procurement, warehousing, logistics, marketing, finance, customer service, etc. To make the right decisions at the right time, information on customer complaints, transactions, production, inventory, sales figures as per past promotions, information on returns, acceptance rate of new product, etc. needs to be made available easily. Along with these internal functions, FirstCry has a vast network of suppliers, franchises and partners. To remain efficient and to respond to business demands as per customers' expectations, competitors' moves, market changes, etc., all the stakeholders need to remain connected to the required information systems. Internal information systems play a critical role in enabling effective decision-making, in avoiding silos and managing collaborations among these multiple stakeholders.

To support FirstCry's continuous business growth and its evolving business models, the company's technology team works in close coordination with the business team, and both business and technology teams understand each other's points of view.

Over a short period of time, FirstCry has had a phenomenal journey. Though FirstCry has become a Goliath in its niche, instead of getting satisfied with what has already been achieved, like David, it keeps on looking for opportunities to solve the unmet needs of parents.

SUPAM MAHESHWARI
fc

Advice from Supam Maheshwari

- Identify a large pain area, build a great team to address that pain area and then execute well.
- Test your concepts first as pilots, get convinced and then scale up.
- Believe in your vision and build a high-performance and ethical work culture.

An enabler of magical change

In today's world, where evolving consumers prefer superior experiences, if you ask anyone what differentiates great brands from average ones, one of the definite answers would be 'design'. But this answer was almost unheard of in 1989, when Ashwini Deshpande and other co-founders started Elephant Design.

Today, Elephant Design is recognised as one of India's topmost independent integrated design consultancy firms. It is now headed by its co-founders Ashwini Deshpande, Ashish Deshpande and Partho Guha. It has won numerous national and international awards, such as eight Rebrand International Awards, Design for Asia Award, Top Design Agency ranking by Economic Times for over eight years, WorldStar Packaging Excellence Award, International A'Design Award, several India Design Marks and many more. It represents India at the Design Alliance Asia, a consortium of design consulting companies across 13 Asian countries. It has more than a hundred clients from almost all business sectors, including many of the fastest-growing startups as well as global market leaders in their respective domains.

From being a college internship project to becoming an internationally recognised design firm, Elephant's dream-to-destiny journey is an inspiring one. It reflects the passion of the team, the evolution of a brand and the creation of a design movement in India.

THE BEGINNING

Ashwini grew up in Aurangabad, a small town in Maharashtra. Along with being good at academics, she was highly inclined towards art, creativity and visual storytelling in school. By 1983, when she was near the end of her schooling, Ashwini realised that she did not want to take up a conventional career path like engineering or medicine. She wasn't fully aware of what a designer did for a career, as there was nobody to find out from. However, due to her inclination towards creativity, she managed to get admission in the National Institute of Design (NID), the premier design institute of India, located in Ahmedabad. During her time in college, she got inspired by companies like Frog Design and Pentagram, global design firms founded in 1969 and 1972 respectively, and some great professors at NID. Over time, she understood the finer elements of design and its purpose.

GETTING THE FIRST CLIENT

Ashwini's entrepreneurial journey began in 1988, while she was doing her internship with the India office of a German multinational conglomerate BASF. Over a period of six months, she helped the company's corporate communication team in designing multiple marketing collaterals such as brochures, calendars, annual reports, etc. She also helped the team design a trade exhibition. During this exhibition, the global corporate communications head of the company happened to be in India and he appreciated the work done by Ashwini. He also saw the other work she had done during her internship and was highly impressed. Eventually, he offered her an opportunity to work on the company's international marketing collaterals such as brochures and corporate audio visuals. Ashwini informed him that she was about to start her own design consultancy with some friends and would be able to take up this project through that firm. He agreed and offered a design fee of around 100,000 Deutsche Marks—that roughly equaled ₹13 lakh in 1989—for the work. Luckily, he needed some time to put things together at his end. So, Ashwini got a grace period of four months to finish her graduation and get her friends to move to Pune to start the company.

BIRTH OF THE BRAND NAME: ELEPHANT DESIGN

As Ashwini had already decided with her batch-mates from NID, there were definitive plans of starting a multidisciplinary design firm soon after graduation. After brainstorming over a name for days, they all seemed to unanimously agree on 'Elephant Design'. The name was inspired by an interesting ancient story about blind men and an elephant.

Once upon a time, in a land far away, lived six blind men. One day they encountered an elephant but had no clue what the creature was. Each one felt a different part of its body and reached his own conclusion. The man who felt a leg thought the animal was like a pillar. The one who felt the elephant's trunk thought it was a tree branch. One of the blind men felt the tail and thought of a rope. All of these men only touched one part of the elephant and began to argue over what the animal really resembled. If you think about it, they all were right in their own way, but they only needed to put their pieces together for the bigger picture—the whole elephant. Similarly, in the world of design, individuals with varied talents and backgrounds bring different perspectives and can collaborate to help an elephant (a richer and bigger picture) emerge. This was the philosophy behind the name. Ashwini and her friends believed in co-creation. They knew that 'design' is a team game, and to be able to make it big they needed to have a collaborative mindset not only among themselves but with their clients, associates and the users of the designs as well.

The name has worked well for the company. It has an excellent recall value, and it also becomes an icebreaker with most new audiences.

BUSINESS LESSONS

There are many important business lessons that can be learnt from the evolution of the brand. A few of them are as follows.

Sell to the right clients

Many startups dream of becoming multimillion-dollar companies quickly and try to do too many things to acquire any kind of clients. On the other hand, there are companies that create a strong position in the market by selectively choosing their market segments and clients. Especially in a B2B consulting business, the quality of clients is more important than quantity. The co-founders of Elephant Design believed that 'design service' is like water. Unless you feel the thirst and need from within, the offering has no value. Since design was an unknown profession in 1989, they set out to create awareness about the profession itself and the benefits of applying design principles to create value. Early on, the co-founders realised that selective clients, who are innovators and early adopters in their respective industries, can not only help the consultancy in building Elephant's credentials, but also provide valuable feedback, new ideas and, based on merit, new references.

Though the company was started after it got its first client, organising revenue from this engagement took some time. Imagine the world in the early 1990s, when there were no communication technologies such as WhatsApp, email and mobile phones. At the time communication across countries was slow, and the back and forth for work took time. Due to a lag in showing the work to the client and getting their feedback, it took almost a year for the team to complete the German project and earn that paycheque. Moreover, during those days, there were no angel investors who could have given money to college graduates for ideas that only existed on paper, and getting a bank loan without collateral was not an option either.

During this one-year period, the team borrowed money from their families to keep them going, managed to complete a few smaller projects and used those funds to buy a slide projector to showcase their college portfolios to prospective clients. As they received the fee from the German client, a large part of it went into buying a computer and a printer. In 1990, Elephant Design was one of the first creative agencies in India to invest in computers that even large advertising agencies had not considered yet. It was clear from the start that they would always invest their profits back into the business.

Even though they didn't have sufficient money, they decided to stay away from meaningless work and focused on getting quality projects that would not only add to their credentials but also demonstrate how design can help in generating value for the client.

Right from the early days, the co-founders immersed themselves in understanding the business landscape of India. They prepared a list of progressive business houses that could become prospective clients where design as a value addition would be easier to demonstrate. To pitch to these prospects, they wrote letters to their founders and CEOs explaining the multidisciplinary nature of their team. Interestingly, an Ahmedabad-based air cooler firm, Symphony, became one of their first clients and remarkably still happens to partner with Elephant Design, more than 25 years later. This not only speaks volumes about the creative abilities of Elephant, but also about the importance the firm gives to building relationships. Over the period, Symphony has grown from a company with a couple of products to a globally recognised leader in evaporative air-cooling with a presence in more than 60 countries. Along with the growth of the client, Elephant's engagement has also evolved from being a design service provider to playing an advisory and strategic role. The Elephant team has been instrumental in designing nearly every product that Symphony has launched in the last 15 years or so, creating new categories such as tall, slim, space-saving or jumbo coolers with better efficiencies and new aesthetics. These designs have played a key role in winning awards, recognitions and, more importantly, increasing sales for the client.

Over a period, the company has worked on experiential branding, packaging and retail projects for some of the leading companies, including Britannia, Procter & Gamble, Unilever, Tata, ICICI, Godrej, MTR and more recently for fast growing startups including Paper Boat, Fingerlix, Epigamia and many more.

Empathise with your customers

Most of the time, companies just focus on the transaction-related part of selling their products and services to customers and forget that every customer is a human being first. Empathy is the art of placing oneself in another's position to understand their experiences, emotions and needs. To do a project well, it is important to identify different personas at your client's end, such as influencers, decision-makers and end users, that is, the client's customers. Every persona has different concerns, expectations and aspirations. At Elephant, walking into the lives of personas to understand their business concerns and life concerns is given utmost importance.

In a B2B engagement, it is not only important to empathise with your client (the manufacturer of products or services), but it is also important to make them empathise with their end consumers (the final users of the products or services). Designers are called users' advocates. Their strength lies in understanding users and their articulated and unarticulated needs. As a part of the process, designers collaborate with the client's R&D teams to understand technology advancements and collaborate with the marketing teams to understand business goals. At Elephant, design teams are always focused on bringing appropriate relevance to the solutions by finding the sweet spot between needs, technology and business.

At the intersection of appropriate technological advances, relevant business goals and understanding the stated and unstated needs of the end consumers lies the sweet spot where success can be created—an outcome that is appreciated by customers and meets business goals.

As an example, Axis Bank, a client of Elephant Design, was moving from bricks-and-mortar to a clicks-and-mortar experience and wanted to launch an Express Branch, a compact

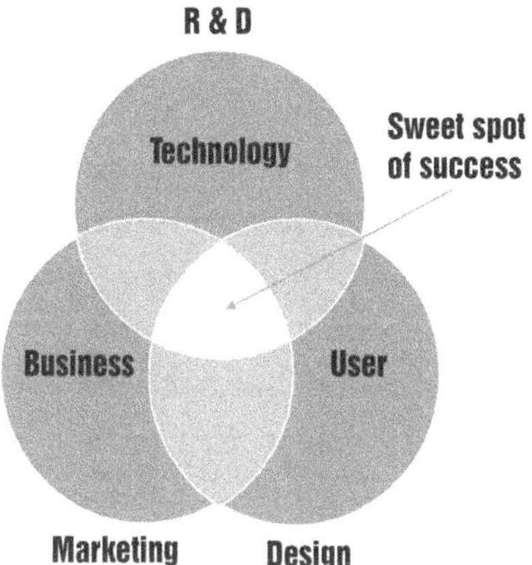

Source: Based on IDEO's Human-Centred Design Toolkit

branch that is conveniently located in malls and offers a superior omni-channel and digital banking experience to today's tech-driven customers.

The Elephant team focused both on their client's business requirement and the end consumers' experience, to design an interactive and efficient retail environment for the branch. Today, these branches play a major role in building and strengthening the bank's relationship with their customers on the go, through an enhanced digital banking experience.

Continuously collect and connect the dots

In his commencement speech at Stanford University, Steve Jobs said, 'You can't connect the dots looking forward; you can only connect them looking backwards. So you have to trust that the dots will somehow connect in your future. You have to trust in something—your gut, destiny, life, karma, whatever. This approach has never let me down, and it has made all the difference in my life.'

Ashwini believes that if one stays curious and involved, then every engagement becomes a unique opportunity to collect new perspectives. This is similar to the analogy of dots and, of course, to the story of the elephant and the blind men as well. She also believes that selective perspectives from one industry or business can be applied to another industry or business to create a highly differentiated, unique experience.

As an interesting example of collecting and connecting the dots, the Elephant team knew of a community of coppersmiths in Pune who create handmade copper utensils. Creating one utensil takes them almost a day and unfortunately, the market for these copper utensils has been decreasing as people have started using stainless steel and glassware. When the Elephant team was working on the design for a unique and culturally relevant baton for the 2008 Commonwealth Youth Games that were held in Pune, they decided to work with this community. The shape of the baton was based on the 'tutari', a local trumpet that was traditionally used to welcome dignitaries. The Elephant team invited the coppersmith community to create a flame-shaped copper leaf for the baton. This baton went around 199 towns for 74 days and around 6,000 sportspersons ran with it. Apart from serving the other objective of promoting sustainable games, this also became a huge awareness initiative for the copper art from Pune.

By working with different types of clients—from startups to established players—in different industries, the Elephant team has created its own collection of dots. They keep on adding new dots to this collection, and pick up relevant dots and connect them to solve their clients' new business challenges.

Promote your category

To create a growing market for your business, you need to educate the market about your category. And to keep on educating the market, you must continually collaborate with like-minded people and upgrade yourself through participating in voluntary initiatives.

Ashwini and her colleagues always viewed design as a catalyst of business growth. As pioneers of the business of design in India, they have helped create awareness about the role of design in creating value and have dispelled several myths about design.

In promoting design, Elephant's unique understanding of culture has played an important role. In the early 2000s, renowned designer William Harald-Wong from Malaysia was visiting India as a board member of a global design association. He got to know that Pune-based Elephant Design had a strong team which had done some path-breaking work for large Indian conglomerates. He visited Pune to meet the team and was impressed by their work rooted in Indian culture.

William had created a consortium called The Design Alliance Asia with the objective of bringing together Asian designers and enabling knowledge exchange between them. He invited the founders of Elephant Design to join the group to represent India. Today, this consortium has designers from 13 Asian countries who meet once every year to discuss and share their insights on global, regional and local design trends. This association has helped Ashwini and her colleagues understand the similarities and differences in various Asian cultures, which in turn has enriched their work. Ashwini is a part of the core group that steers the consortium. This has also given her the opportunity to play a key role in a collaborative research project titled 'Colours of Asia' that was supported by the Hong Kong government. Ashwini has also edited a book with the same title, which was awarded Design for Asia Special Culture Award.

Because of its deep understanding of culture and beliefs, Elephant has been the go-to choice for many global businesses when they are looking to develop specific products or services for India. Some of them include Bharat Benz, Gillette, Nissan Motors and Liebherr.

To promote design in India and enable the exchange of good practices among designers, Ashwini and her colleagues have collaborated with designers in Pune and facilitated the creation of the Pune Design Foundation. In 2005, it evolved into the Association of Designers in India, a professional not-for-profit body of designers and design organisations in India. Since 2006, along with her fabulous team, Ashwini has been instrumental in organising various activities, including the Pune Design Festival, with the aim to spread awareness about design. As the President of the Association of Designers of India (2017-18), Elephant co-founder Ashish Deshpande ensured design representation at the highest policy level.

There is not much literature on design available in regional languages. In an attempt to remedy this, and to spread awareness about the value of design in the daily lives of common people, Ashwini has been writing a fortnightly column in the Marathi newspaper *Sakal*.

Ashwini suggests that one should give importance to every single opportunity and prepare for it thoroughly. When people see your conviction, they either join you in making things happen or they connect you to other relevant people, and one thing leads to another. So, in a sense, no opportunity is big or small. It is what you make of it.

Along with creating awareness, Elephant has also been focused on making a social impact through design. Ashwini was invited by The Rockefeller Foundation to participate in a Global Social Impact summit in 2008. She came back from their Bellagio (Italy) campus with three learnings:

1. Social Impact can start in your backyard. You don't need to start with large problems to make a difference.
2. Everybody wants to do good. So, a social impact project can piggyback on a commercial project for reach and financial efficiency.
3. You (and your business) can do well by doing good.

Ashwini and her colleagues have tried to implement these learnings into everything they do at Elephant. Right from being a zero-wet-waste company to helping local communities to giving identity to socially relevant initiatives like the Pune Bus Day, Britannia Nutrition Foundation, de Asra Foundation, etc., Ashwini has played an instrumental role in establishing a global footprint for Indian design. She has lectured in more than 20 countries and represented Indian design and culture. She has been a jury member at Cannes Lions (France), Global ReBrand 100 (USA), Spikes Asia (Singapore), Design for Asia (Hong Kong), Kyiv International Advertising Festival (Ukraine), Design for Change (India) Awards and International A'Design Awards (Italy).

As a business leader in the creative industry, Ashwini has won many accolades. She has been on the 50 Most Influential Women in Media in India list of *Impact* magazine for three consecutive years. She was conferred the Leader of the Decade Award by All Ladies League at the Women Economic Forum in Delhi, and the Mayor of Pune city presented her the Amrutwel Foundation's SuperWoman 2017 Award.

With a focus on promoting the business of design, she has not only created awareness about the profession but has also become a personal brand herself, though that was never her intention.

Design your culture

An organisation's brand is dependent on the quality of work done by its team members. When the team feels empowered, it always boosts the end result. As the organisation grows, both its employees and clients increase in numbers. For its employees to do more and to do it better, it is important to focus on developing a culture that encourages positive behaviour and actions. To facilitate the development of such a culture in the company, the leaders must be approachable and must play a keen and active role in their teams' development and growth.

Ashwini and the leadership at Elephant believe in building a strong next line of leadership within the organisation. Ashwini always encourages her team members to speak at various forums, become a part of the jury in design competitions and participate in design-related events. Being an established designer, many such opportunities come her way, but she believes it is important to share the glory with promising team members who may make the future leadership of the company.

With a focus on creating ownership and executing multiple projects with defined quality benchmarks, Elephant has created decentralised teams that take ownership of projects and are empowered to define timelines, speed and innovation for their projects. Like mini startups within the system, these decentralised teams push themselves to give their best to their projects and get the credit for the outcome.

Ashwini believes that all great ideas can't come from the top, and everyone in an organisation should get a chance to share their ideas. For more than 15 years now, Elephant Design has had a ritual of a Monday Morning Meeting where the entire team spends an hour together. This becomes an opportunity for everyone to meet and for one of the team members to speak, conduct a workshop or organise a group activity. This is also a forum where the leadership gets a chance to consistently discuss the Elephant values and keep everyone on the same page.

At Elephant, it is believed that the focus on an individual's growth leads to the team's growth and the growth of multiple teams leads to the organisation's growth. The ambitions of every individual change with time, and they must be nurtured to grow in the right direction. At Elephant, individual goals are aligned with team goals, and the goals of the various teams are aligned with those of the organisation. Goals that are not aligned get filtered during the process. This helps team members move in a direction that leads to Elephant's business growth as well as helps the members grow themselves.

Don't dilute your brand

Most of the time, organisations think that growth means gaining more clients, more revenue and more market share. To achieve this growth aspiration, they extend their well-respected brand name to newer domains without thinking about whether these align with the core values and capabilities of the brand. In the short run, they might be able to gain some more market share based on the credibility of their brand, but in the long run their brand may get diluted if the delivery quality in the new domain is not at par with past credibility.

Elephant has been very selective in defining its growth. Instead of using its brand name to get into new domains and becoming a generalist, it has focused on enhancing respect and expanding the market for its specialised category, that is, design-led innovation. Over a period, along with services such as communication design, industrial design, environment design and packaging design, it has started providing more value-added services such as design research, innovation strategy and brand strategy to its clients. These value additions have helped increase both its revenue and reputation.

Because of its high-quality work, many of the company's clients have become its brand advocates. For over 15 years, Elephant has got all of its work because of word-of-mouth publicity through its existing clients or associates. Moreover, when individuals at Elephant's clients move from one organisation to another, they recommend the firm in their new organisations. To keep the promise of high-end quality intact, the company must make sure that its employees remain excited about new projects and give their best. The company has been selective in picking up the projects and for every new project, it applies a three-criteria filter: earning, learning and excitement. At least two of the criteria must be met for a project to be considered worthy of investing the time and effort of the team.

Design is an integral part of branding strategy. It elevates the perception of a brand and creates differentiation. But perhaps due to the lack of awareness about branding and design firms, most companies have traditionally relied more on mass advertising for brand creation. However, with the market changing rapidly, attention spans are reducing drastically and the number of choices is ever-increasing. To differentiate themselves and provide meaningful experiences to their customers, many companies are now waking up to design as a key differentiator in their strategies.

On another note, increasing awareness about design has also led to a growth in the number of educational institutes in India that are focusing on design and creating a great supply of talent.

The self-explanatory infographic by Elephant Design shows how design plays an important role in business.

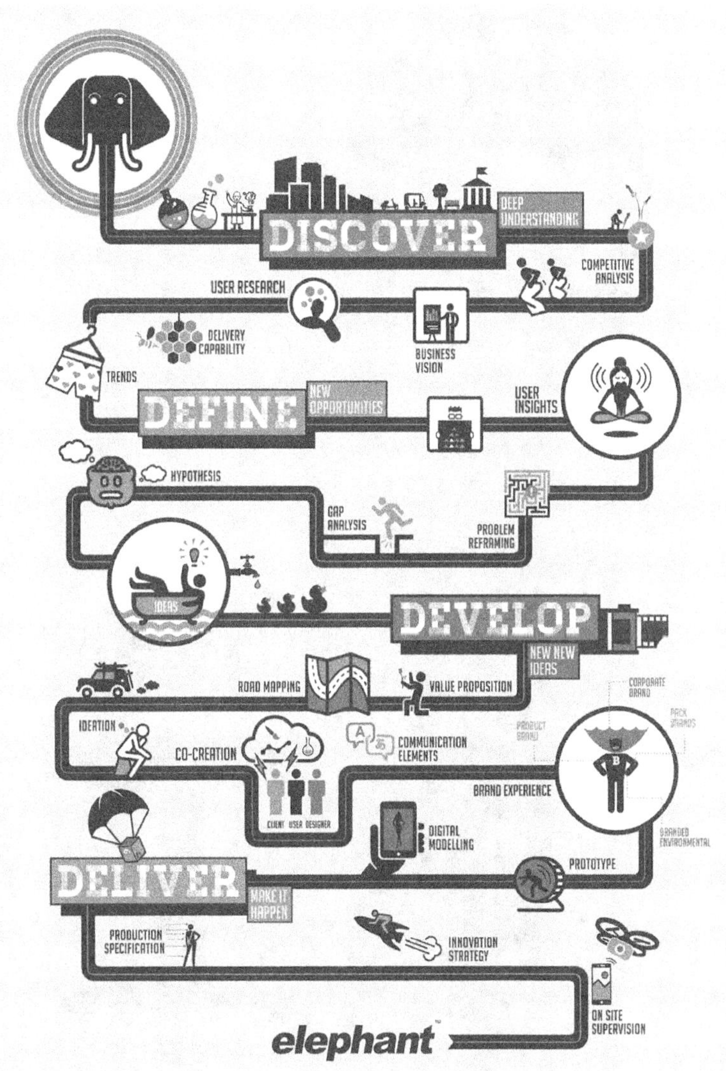

Source: Elephant Design

ASHWINI DESHPANDE

Over a period, many international players have entered the Indian design market, many boutique design consulting companies have opened and many marketing agencies have opened design arms. 'The more the better,' says Ashwini, as the presence of more players will help in creating awareness about design as a profession, and clients will also understand how to derive better value out of design. Ashwini believes that India needs at least a hundred large and professionally managed design consulting firms like Elephant to be able to see a positive difference in the economy as well as the daily lives of people.

Advice from Ashwini Deshpande

- Designers cannot behave like gods. They cannot assume they know everything. They need to be able to understand specific situations with utmost empathy and without any prejudices.
- Give yourself a new challenge every now and then and once you overcome that challenge, put another challenge in front of you. Thrive on challenges.
- Focus on creating magical and meaningful experiences for your clients. When you do honest and impactful work, not only will the end users benefit, but your clients will become your brand ambassadors too.
- Don't ignore industry trends and your competition (both contextual and non-contextual). Companies like Nokia and Kodak couldn't sustain their leadership position because they ignored a non-contextual company like Apple that unexpectedly took their market by surprise.
- It is important to stay relevant and appropriate in the Indian context where even basic necessities are luxuries to many.

Unlocking massive value by connecting entrance exam aspirants

The world of entrepreneurship has always had individuals who have been called crazy by the people around them. These entrepreneurs see things differently, are not fond of rules and have the guts to challenge the status quo. One such entrepreneur is Allwin Agnel. While doing his B.Com., he decided to foray into the internet industry. This was the time when the world was going through a dot-com bust that had ended many internet startups.

A serial entrepreneur, Allwin has created many ventures in the internet space. One of his creations is known as PaGaLGuY. com. Ask anyone connected with India's MBA entrance examinations, be it students or teachers at coaching classes, or professors at business schools, they would have surely come across PaGaLGuY. Started in 2002 as an MBA education community, the platform has turned into a social network and has expanded to many other entrance exam sub-communities like banking, engineering, medicine and civil services.

Every year, over 10 million users visit PaGaLGuY and many of them are active on PaGaLGuY's discussion threads. The site gets over 300 million page views and over 3 million comments annually. Today, PaGaLGuY is considered India's largest education network and a pioneer in the space of online communities. Like a few other online brands such as Facebook, Twitter and Wikipedia, PaGaLGuY has also changed the way people generate and consume content, communicate and help each other.

Interestingly, Allwin continued his studies while running his business. He completed his M.Com. and after turning his business profitable in 2006, he went to the prestigious Wharton School in the USA for MBA. While at Wharton, Allwin managed his company remotely with the support of his wonderful team in India. Allwin is also a private pilot and the winner of the Ford Fellowship award given to people who have researched and published papers on disruptive technologies.

This chapter recounts the inspiring journey of PaGaLGuY, from its unexpected beginnings to its astonishing heights.

THE BEGINNING OF THE JOURNEY

In the early 2000s, when he was a commerce student at Mumbai University, Allwin co-founded a web hosting company called Neutral Web. He arranged the funds for the company using a credit card loan. Everybody thought Allwin was crazy for trying to do something in the area of technology without having any technical qualifications. Eventually, the venture failed. But before it did, Allwin had managed to grow Neutral Web's clients base to over 18 countries.

This was also the era when an MBA qualification was very popular and the exam preparation space was unorganised. In the Indian context, engineering students used to dominate the MBA entrance exams. There was hardly any forum for students from other backgrounds such as commerce to get their queries resolved and connect with engineering students for information exchange. One day, a friend from his graduation days was sharing his disappointment about the lack of organised information on business school applications and preparation material with Allwin. Being exposed to the power of the internet, Allwin felt he could help many aspiring students like his friend by starting an online community.

With an investment of ₹20,000, he started a hobby project—an online community where aspirants could discuss everything related to MBA entrance exams.

BIRTH OF THE BRAND NAME: PaGaLGuY

The Hindi word 'Pagal' is commonly used to refer to people who are eccentric and are considered misfits. In the early 2000s, technology was considered high-end and comprehensible only to engineers. During this period, when Allwin, a commerce student, spoke about technology, people around him didn't take him seriously. Unable to understand why he was taking so much interest in technology instead of commerce, many of his friends called him pagal.

Because he became famous as a pagal guy in his social circle, Allwin bought the domain name pagalguy.com and even created an email address to match—me@pagalguy.com. This was an era when Yahoo mail was quite popular and Gmail was not even in existence. Creating an email ID on a personally purchased domain name was almost unheard of, especially from a commerce student in India. Again, people felt Allwin was spending money on his foolish interests and called him crazy. But they remembered his unique email address.

When Allwin started an online community to help MBA aspirants, he was looking for a domain name. Due to low internet penetration in India and a lack of interest from people in this kind of discussion forum, he felt his idea might not work. To test his idea, instead of buying a new domain name, he thought of using the previously purchased domain name Pagalguy. com. When someone is trying to do something interesting and different, he has to be a little pagal to persistently work towards his aspiration. Allwin felt this name might connect well with MBA aspirants as they were trying to do something different and interesting by preparing for a highly competitive exam like CAT.

The name Pagalguy.com resonated with MBA aspirants, and the online community quickly gained popularity. When he noticed the popularity of the name PaGaLGuY, which he had so far considered to be a temporary one, Allwin decided to retain it for his new business.

BUSINESS LESSONS

There are many important business lessons that can be learnt from the evolution of this brand created by Allwin. A few of them are as follows.

Build stickiness into your product

In this context, stickiness in a product means that the users of a product want to keep coming back to use it. Stickiness is also a measure of how well a brand resonates with its consumers. There are many reasons for users to stick to PaGaLGuY.

Firstly, users join PaGaLGuY for a common purpose, that is, entrance exam preparation. There are multiple entrance exams and for each exam, students have various queries about subjects, application processes, exam experience and so on. A discussion by a few users about any topic generates a lot of content, which becomes useful for many others. Because of the presence of like-minded people in the community, more and more people join the community and keep on returning to consume the information. This leads to strong network effects.

Secondly, because the messages on various discussion threads are archived, it is possible for new users to go through even decade-old discussions by previous users on useful topics. As many new aspirants go through similar challenges that were faced by others in the past, the archived information acts as a goldmine for new users.

Thirdly, entrance exams are highly competitive in nature. When students are preparing for such exams, they want someone who can solve their queries quickly and help them move ahead in their journey. Interestingly, the people who compete with each other in exams become invisible online friends on PaGaLGuY and help one another. Based on their contributions over time, active users build credibility and respect within the community. When people are seen helping each other, more and more people come forward to assist one another, and because of the combined effect of this movement everybody in the community benefits.

The availability of a lot of helpful information in one place allows existing users to become evangelists of the community and bring in more users through word of mouth. Moreover, in the case of many products that are transactional in nature, switching costs involve monetary discomfort. But for products like PaGaLGuY, switching cost involves psychological and emotional discomfort caused by the loss of identification and relationships. Therefore, users prefer to stick to the community and continue to add value and consume information.

Focus on being 'much better' rather than being 'just better'

Every business has competitors, and to gain market share, the business tries to make its product a little better than those of its competitors. If a brand is only marginally better than its competitors, then its competitors can catch up within a few months. But if a brand is much better than its competitors, then it becomes difficult for its competitors to catch up. For example, though Google was a late entrant in the search industry, it came up with a much better product and none of the existing competitors were able to catch up to Google.

Along with competition, the brand must keep in mind changing consumer behaviour. Technology is evolving very fast and consumers are continuously getting exposed to new things. Even if its competitors are not catching up, if a brand doesn't reinvent itself, consumers can move on to something more advanced. For example, in the case of digital cameras, consumers moved on from using brands like Canon and Nikon to using smartphones that came up with powerful cameras.

Interestingly, during the initial years of PaGaLGuY, social networks like Facebook and Twitter were not in existence and people used to interact through Yahoo Groups or mails. Since it is an online community, the way that PaGaLGuY organised the discussion threads and aggregated information gave it an edge with users who found it to be a better place to connect than other platforms like Yahoo Groups, or limiting themselves to one-on-one communication through emails. Within a short span of time, PaGaLGuY became a popular website.

Jack Ma said, 'Most companies, when they're doing good, they enjoy today's wonderful life. They don't worry about five years later—but I worry about five years later.' Similarly, rather than being satisfied with the phenomenal growth of his idea, Allwin kept on updating his product based on evolving user behaviour, technology trends and new features of internet-based businesses. By the time users got exposed to social networks like Facebook and Twitter, PaGaLGuY had already evolved from an online community to a social network which let users create profiles, chat on forums and participate in offline meetups. Later, developments like the availability of Wi-Fi connections, fast internet connections, and the increased usage of smartphones contributed to the change in the behaviour of internet users. By the time users arrived in the new era, the PaGaLGuY team was ready with its user-friendly mobile application.

To stay ahead of the competition, the PaGaLGuY team continuously reinvents the product by adopting emerging technologies. Also, to accommodate any changes in user behaviour, the team keeps on imagining how the future would be and continuously innovates the product to remain ready, before the user even arrives in the future.

Look for organic ways to increase your user base

Philip Kotler said, 'Don't buy market share. Figure out how to earn it.' Interestingly, PaGaLGuY is one of those unconventional brands that has never advertised itself through paid channels. Its user base has grown organically through word of mouth.

When Allwin started PaGaLGuY in 2002, there were limited websites on the internet, and there was hardly any online community that focused on education. To get the initial set of users, Allwin sent messages to various Yahoo Groups where students would discuss MBA-related stuff. Many of the early adopters of PaGaLGuY came through this route. Later, they brought in more users through word of mouth. Moreover, at that time only news-related sites used to be rich in content, and websites based on user-generated content were not in vogue yet. Because of the user-generated content in the form of comments and information on various business schools, PaGaLGuY became a content-rich website very quickly. Because of this, it used to get ranked higher by search engines. And by appearing in the top search results for MBA-related keywords, it attracted more users.

Thanks to its MBA-focused user base, many business school students started approaching PaGaLGuY to become their media partner and market their annual festivals. In return, PaGaLGuY got a significant presence through booths and banners at almost all major business school festivals in India. Many engineering students participate in these festivals. They got to know about the brand and spread the word in their colleges. In a few years, participation by engineering students grew by leaps and bounds. Quickly, members of the PaGaLGuY community started meeting in person in various cities and this meeting platform evolved as PaGaLGuY Meets followed by an annual event—All India PaGaLGuY Meet—which became an offline platform for various business school students and aspirants to connect with each other.

Over time, students in MBA colleges spoke about the community with their professors and suggested that they join it to listen to the voice of MBA aspirants. Earlier, there was some resistance from college representatives to join an unofficial community with a weird name, but they realised that many students were present on the community and if colleges didn't participate in these discussions, students may move on to other colleges. Eventually, the college staff started joining the community. Soon, PaGaLGuY became a platform for colleges to learn about their aspirants' mindsets, queries and challenges. For aspirants too, it became a great forum to discuss their queries with the college staff and look into the discussions of others.

In 2009, PaGaLGuY launched India's largest B-school rankings initiative and released its annual B-school ranking charts based on crowdsourced surveys taken by over 9,500 MBA students as well as alumni. Later, PaGaLGuY launched an MBA Apply programme, allowing students to register on the website and apply to multiple colleges through a single platform. Through this programme, the status of an application could be tracked, the student could correspond with an institute and pay the application fee.

Because of its optimised website design and availability of useful information, users spend a lot of time on the website. Due to its niche user base, PaGaLGuY acts as a highly targeted advertising platform for various businesses in the education space, and hence receives a lot of relevant views.

Create a sense of belonging among brand users

The American psychologist Abraham Harold Maslow said that 'belonging' was one of the five basic human needs. When people get an emotional pay-off for being associated with a brand, they develop a sense of belonging to that brand.

Preparing for a competitive exam is a tough and lonely journey in which aspirants face many ups and downs. PaGaLGuY has become a positive influence in this journey of loneliness, by creating an opportunity for like-minded people across the country to connect, share their experiences and make new experiences with each other. Users can broadcast their feelings and connect with other users with similar experiences. This makes them realise that they are not alone and that other students are going through similar challenges.

It's a well-known fact that people remember their days of struggle and the people who helped them during that period. Through PaGaLGuY, users can connect with other users who help them, motivate them and share useful information. Users visualise PaGaLGuY as something more than just a product. It is considered a part of their everyday lives during preparation. It is an independent platform where they can share anything and everything related to their experiences with different coaching classes, multiple exams, interviews, colleges and so on.

Due to the presence of a lot of data and interaction with students in various forums, the team has been able to develop a superior understanding of its user base by applying techniques of big data analysis and humanities. This understanding helps the team further enhance the product and meet the unmet demands of the users. For example, through analysis, the team found that, in line with the 90-9-1 rule pertaining to participation in an internet community, only 1 per cent of the users of a website actively participate, create new content and become power users, 9 per cent of the participants tend to be irregular participants who post once a while, while the balance 90 per cent of the participants only view the content and don't contribute. With this insight, the team came up with multiple ways to keep various segments of the user base engaged and active.

Within a community, a tribe gets formed when a leader emerges, sets the direction and then facilitates ways for the tribe to connect and move forward together. At PaGaLGuY, these kinds of tribes are present in the form of active threads, which are led by 1 per cent of the members, the ones that are highly active within the community. It is their passion that draws other users towards a thread. To reward these highly active members and keep them engaged, the company uses gamification techniques such as achievement badges. These recognitions help active participants gain respect among millions of other participants. This elevated status in the community makes active participants known among other students not only in the online world, but also in the offline world when they join their colleges or come to PaGaLGuY meets. This popularity makes them feel happy and further motivates them to lead new tribes in the future.

We all have a basic need to connect with other human beings and make friends. When we connect with others during a common journey, we develop a relationship that is especially useful at some point in our life. Students would have gone to different coaching classes, joined different colleges as per entrance scores, and could be from anywhere and any background, but they all would have been on PaGaLGuY. Because they have been a part of the same community, students have many common memories and experiences.

By being a part of students' journeys of preparation for competitions, PaGaLGuY has become a part of their memories that bring excitement, pleasure and nostalgia of those days of struggle. They remember PaGaLGuY as a platform that helped them move their career forward by facilitating all the required support from many invisible online friends.

Empower your team

Many companies fail to understand what motivates people, and they try outdated methods of monetary incentives and gifts. Very early in his journey, Allwin discovered that small rewards like incentives and gifts provide only short-term motivation. However, an approach that involves instilling a sense of purpose, positive feedback and empowerment can have long-term impact. He also realised that empowered teams accept increased levels of accountability for the work they do.

When Allwin went for his MBA to the USA between 2006 and 2008, his two-member team not only ran the whole business in his absence but took the company to profitability. When he returned, his startup had already grown to a 15-member team. Along with empowering the team, a leader has to gain the respect and support of his team members. After completing his MBA, Allwin had multiple opportunities in the USA. But he had promised his team members that he would re-join them after his MBA. He kept his promise and came back to India. His sense of purpose lay beyond making money, which further inspired his team members.

When a leader is open to new ideas and opinions from team members, team members feel more empowered. At PaGaLGuY, the team members collaborate not for money, nor for any rewards, but for the sake of innovation, progress and accomplishment. To make sure that users follow the community guidelines, the team moderates the forum through analytics, automation and machine-learning–based tools. Based on analyses, the team continuously comes up with new ideas. For instance, when the team observed a rise in discussions related to Bank PO and UPSC exams on the community, they discussed with Allwin and made many new sub-communities within PaGaLGuY. These sub-communities helped to further increase the highly segmented user base.

PaGaLGuY is one of the premium publishers in the online advertising industry. To maintain its standards, the sales team makes sure that they don't sell ad space inventory to any irrelevant advertisers. Moreover, they don't hard sell the ad space either. They consider what is right for the users, advertisers and company from a relationship and positioning perspective and take decisions accordingly. Their incentives depend not on their sales numbers but on the relevance of the advertisements for the members of the community.

Allwin says, 'PaGaLGuY faced many challenges in terms of growth and staffing, but over a period of time we were able to learn from mistakes and grow.' Because of its work culture and popularity among college graduates, every year around 10,000 to 12,000 aspirants apply to PaGaLGuY for jobs, but Allwin has been very selective in creating his team and hires only 10 to 12 people from the applicants.

In his book, *It Happened in India*, Kishore Biyani said, 'When one is young and tries to rewrite rules, he is called mad. But when he is finally successful, because he dared to risk it, he is called a maverick.' Allwin's journey is a testament to this statement. When he started his entrepreneurial journey, people around him called him mad (pagal), but today he is called a maverick who created a one-of-a-kind education-based social network in the world. To get into the next orbit of growth, Allwin is continuously enhancing PaGaLGuY and starting new ventures in the education space.

ALLWIN AGNEL

Advice from Allwin Agnel

- The startup journey is challenging as an entrepreneur has to deal with issues they haven't faced before. To traverse this journey, you need to find amazing people to work with who will support you during tough times and allow you to dream bigger.
- Don't build solutions that make sense only in the present. You should always imagine how the future will be and then build solutions that consider the future.
- The job of technology is to make people's lives simpler. Focus on creating user-friendly products that, through their simplicity, can solve complex problems in users' lives.
- Nothing is certain, always keep experimenting.
- Think of your brand as a tool that can solve your users' problems and align with their emotions and feelings.

Acknowledgements

This book would not have been possible without the advice, motivation and support of some incredible people who contributed immensely to my endeavour.

I would first and foremost like to thank my wife Pooja. Ever since I conceived the idea of writing this book, she has been my pillar of strength. She listened to my ideas, shared valuable feedback and helped me structure my thoughts. On weekends and holidays, as I utilised every minute of my personal time to complete this project, she sacrificed her plans and kept my morale high with her positive thoughts. She also helped me focus and brought a lot of discipline to my work, without which I couldn't have completed this book.

Though I had written many articles in the past, writing a book was a totally new experience for me. I am thankful to Saaz Aggarwal, who listened to me patiently and helped me in strategising my approach.

I am thankful to Anand Lunia for being an extraordinary supporter of this journey of mine. He always kept my morale high and made me believe that I could do it.

I am grateful to Arvind Kishore for his encouragement and invaluable help in reviewing the manuscript. His feedback on the early drafts helped me improve my writing. I would also like to thank my friends Jay Prakash Jha and Jason Rodrigues for their inputs.

I deeply appreciate the support of Vivek Singh, Sudhir Syal, Milap Shah, Gaurav Mendiratta and Shripad Nadkarni who were generous with their help. Thanks to Vinay Joy, Swarup Nanda, Sharanya Ranga and Sameer Arora for supporting me in everything I do. I am deeply grateful to Arpit Jain, Manish Acharya, Achintya Goyal and Devendra Khatri for their invaluable assistance.

A big thank you to the founders and the teams of all the companies covered in this book. They gave me their valuable time and shared their journeys with a lot of passion and patience. At Goli Vada Pav, thanks to Venkatesh Iyer and Brijesh Singh; at BookMyShow, thanks to Ashish Hemrajani and Arushi Maheshwari; at Shaadi.com, thanks to Anupam Mittal, Gourav Rakshit and Kayshel Fernandes; at Jayaashree Industries, thanks to Arunachalam Muruganantham; at Su-Kam, thanks to Kunwer Sachdev and Shivani Kashyap; at BYJU'S thanks to Byju Raveendran, Divya Gokulnath, Arjun Mohan and Sanghamitra Bhargov; at FirstCry, thanks to Supam Maheshwari; at PaGaLGuY, thanks to Allwin Agnel; at Elephant Design, thanks to Ashwini Deshpande; at Hector Beverages (Paper Boat), thanks to Neeraj Kakkar and Parvesh Debuka; at Zomato, thanks to Deepinder Goyal, Pankaj Chaddah and Pramod Rao.

I am thankful to Prashant Sinha and his team for creating wonderful caricatures of the founders covered in the book.

I express my utmost gratitude to the entire team at TV18 Broadcast Limited (CNBC TV18) for publishing the first edition of this book. I am also grateful to Westland Books for recognising the potential of my work and agreeing to publish this edition. A special thanks to Karthika V.K. for her invaluable guidance and unwavering support. I deeply appreciate the tremendous support of Sonia Madan in this project. Thank you, Sonia, for making this book so much better with your thoughtful edits. I also want to thank Avdyushka Gupta for her round of edits and proofreading.

Finally, I would like to thank the countless people who have helped shape my journey. I am thankful to Manak Singh and Zankhana Kaur for giving me an opportunity to work at TiE. I am also thankful to R. Sriram, Ajit Nagral, Vispy Doctor, Hareesh Tibrewala, Anuj Jain and Mohit Dubey, for inspiring me to build a career in marketing. Thanks to Sandeep Singhal, Sasha Mirchandani, Sourav Majumdar, Hariharan M. and Prakash Iyer, for inspiring me to become an author. Thanks to Raj Nair, Arun Diaz, Pramod Gothi, Sumir Verma, Mahesh Krishnamurti, Pravin Gandhi, Lakshmi Pratury, Kanchan Kumar, Shabnam Khan, Rahul Tewari, Gautam Sharma, Nitin Seth, Vibhu Nagral, Ajay Hattangdi, Mahalakshmi Ajaykumar, Aashika Jain and my sister Honey, for encouraging me to pursue meaningful goals.